THE SUCCESSFUL Coaching MANAGER

Allan Mackintosh BSc FInstSMM

The Successful Coaching Manager

A manager's guide to coaching individuals and teams effectively

Published by
Matador
12 Manor Walk, Coventry Road
Market Harborough
Leics LE16 9BP, UK
Tel: (+44) 1858 468828 / 469898
Email: books@troubador.co.uk
Web: www.troubador.co.uk/matador

ISBN 1 899293 64 7

Typesetting: Troubador Publishing Ltd, Market Harborough, UK
Printed and bound by Publish on Demand

Matador is an imprint of Troubador Publishing Ltd

Contents

Introduction

Welcome to *The Successful Coaching Manager*. This book is dedicated to all the hard working managers in business worldwide who have people to lead and manage. Managing and leading individuals and teams of individuals can be one of the most satisfying roles there is but on the other hand it can be one of the most stressful, particularly if the skills of the manager are lacking and the company isn't providing the ongoing support and development that is required to continually support and increase the effectiveness of it's managers.

This is a practical handbook, designed to support the hard working manager of today. I have kept it short and concise but you will find it is packed with useful theories and models from traditional works but also backed up by my own considerable management experience. I have selected models and approaches that have worked for me and my fellow coaches and managers and my aim is to bring effective coaching to the role of managers. Coaching is a wonderful skill that can transform the lives of the coached and the coaching manager.

The manager who coaches effectively empowers people to dramatically improve their performance at work. This benefits everyone: the organisation, the manager, the team, and the person being coached. After eight years experience as a specialised coach within industry, I am now currently working in my own management coaching business and it brings me great pleasure to share with you the knowledge and experience that has come as a result of twenty-one years of managing and of being managed.

Management is a really tough game. I call it a game because some managers "play" at it, and a portion of those who do take it seriously always want to win for themselves. Still others are determined to do their best for their people, their organisation, and themselves. Those managers, whose aim is for the latter, are the ones who will succeed. This book will help you become a better manager, by helping you develop in one area of management: coaching. There are many other facets to management, but the skill of dealing with people whether it is an employee, the "boss," or a customer, is by far the toughest skill to develop, but it also brings the greatest rewards.

Many industries are investigating ways to help their managers coach more effectively. This is partly due to the success sports coaches have on motivational and developmental growth of their athletes. It is recognised that top business people have skills similar to the sports coach that could be used to achieve similar results with employees in businesses.

This book will give you ideas, some "do's and don'ts," and real life examples that demonstrate the best ways to coach in a management and team environment. It will not, however, enable you to become an effective coach just by reading it. To truly master the skill of a "great coach," and become a successful coaching manager, it will be necessary for you to be able to convert theory into practice, and continue to practice your skills, as well as continually ask for feedback from people you work with. Having your own coach will help you develop your own coaching skills even more quickly.

Enjoy.

Allan Mackintosh
Professional Management Coach
allan@pmcscotland.com

Acknowledgements

I would like to acknowledge all those managers I have had the pleasure (and in some cases displeasure) of working with since 1982. Without your combination of expertise, skill and in some cases incompetence, this work would never have been possible!

To Landie Van Haren (*www.bridgewaymarketing.com*), Writing Consultant and Business Coach, for editing and marketing support associated with the forerunner of this book, the e-book, *The Coaching Manager*.

To Sean Weafer, the President of The International College of Coaching and Mentoring who, over a pint of Guinness in Dublin, gave me both "food for thought" and ideas in relation to the final format of this book.

Finally to my wife, Shirley, my son, Kerr and daughter, Heather whose patience enabled me to find time to write it and whose impatience made sure that I didn't burn too much midnight oil!

Allan Mackintosh
May 2003

PART I

The Coaching Manager and Individuals

CHAPTER 1

What is Coaching?

Coaching is a wonderful skill, which if used appropriately by managers can transform the lives of both the manager and the person being coached. Coaching unlocks a person's potential in order to maximise performance.

Coaching is only part of the manager's responsibilities and the challenge of management is to ensure that all the aspects of management are built into that role. It is important to promote the skill of coaching, but without the other aspects of management a manager would not be fully effective in the role.

Managers must ensure that they use a balance of all skills to be successful. Other aspects may include recruitment, performance management, financial management, business planning, and a lot of other duties not covered here. This book will only address the development of the manager's role as coach. Being a successful coach does not guarantee managerial success. I know; I've been there. Even though it is not the only component, it is an extremely important one, and one which should be developed if you want to be successful.

The challenge of coaching as I have experienced it in the eight years I have been coaching business people is that of managers struggling to cope with it, both in terms of learning the skills and also taking the time to put them into practice. Managers' excuses for why they don't or won't coach vary enormously. One common reason is "It's easier and less time consuming to tell them what to do," and another reply I have heard is, "I am here to manage, not to coach." Probably the worst comment I heard is, "These people do not deserve a coach." There will be more information about beliefs in a later chapter.

Coach training courses have helped to give people some initial exposure to the skill of coaching, but the challenge occurs when the course is over and there is no qualified coaching support available for follow-up. In a later chapter we will look at the reasons why coaching skills are not assimilated into practice as well as they should be.

Sir John Whitmore, performance coach and best selling author on the subject recognises this problem, too. In his book, *Coaching for Performance*, he says,

> "... the hunger for coaching has resulted in hastily and inadequately trained managers, or so called coaches, failing to meet the expectations of those they are coaching. Too many times they have not fully understood the performance related, psychological principals on which coaching are based."
> (Whitmore, 2).

How true! Thinking back to the early days, in my case this was *very* true. I was thrown into coaching at a time of extreme organisational change. Training was given and although some of it stuck, the majority of it was lost in the need to get things done, within the task-oriented culture of the organisation I worked for at the time. It was not until I experienced expert coaching from an external independent coach that I learned and experienced the power of good coaching. It had taken me thirteen years and many managers before I experienced the effects of excellent coaching. It really did change the way I look at life and my approach to it.

The longest journey begins with the first steps. For a coach the first step should be: clarifying in your own mind exactly what coaching is. We are all aware that there are coaches in sports and sometimes that is where the initial confusion starts. A lot of coaches in sports are actually not true coaches, but trainers. Some trainers shout a lot, direct, and pass on advice, advice that is usually based on their own knowledge and experience. Good coaches are self-aware; they listen intently, question appropriately, and challenge assumptions and actions. They will direct, but only when appropriate, and they only use their own knowledge and experience when they know it will move the people they coach forward.

In my own experience one of the main differences between a good coach and a directive trainer or manager is the coach does not make judgments and does not let ego get in the way. Coaching is intended to enhance the performance of others through feedback, motivation, effective listening, and questioning. Above all, coaching aims to enable the coached to do it on their own!

People get confused between coaching and training and coaching and mentoring. Some others think coaching is therapy of some sort and that only "remedials" need coaching. The difference between coaching and training is that coaching asks questions and is, in the main, non-directive. Training is mostly directive and involves giving people information and skills. There is a saying that "Coaching delivers what Training can only promise" and this I find to be very true. Coaching in fact is a fantastic way of ensuring the skills and learns of training are sustained. Mentoring is more directive than non-directive and usually involves a senior person giving a junior the benefit of their experience through the giving of advice. Coaching is also not counselling as coaching is future orientated and action based whereas counselling tends to be very much about the present and the past and tends to centre on issues, which tend to be of a very personal nature. Managers should not get themselves into a counselling situation unless they are fully qualified in counselling skills. Otherwise they should refer employees onwards if there is any evidence the employee needs counselling.

Take Action

My own definition of coaching is that it is a highly developed skill that embraces active listening, appropriate questioning, and feedback in order to motivate an individual towards enhanced productivity and well being, but there are numerous definitions of coaching. I advise you to go out and do some reading on the subject. Go to your company or local library, search the web, or speak to a coach if you know one. Make sure you understand what coaching is, what coaches do, and what skills coaches and managers need to coach effectively. These skills will be covered in this book although it is always wise to look at other sources on coaching to get a range of perspectives.

When you are ready for training why not talk to your boss and see if your company offers assistance with training? There may be money available in a Training or Personal Development Budget. Enroll in a coach-training course or you could hire your own personal coach. The links below will direct you to resources to help you find training courses and coaches. It is vital that you get a full understanding of what coaching is about and where it fits in the overall scheme of management.

Try these: *www.pmcscotland.com*
               www.coachgraduate.com
               www.coachville.com
               www.coachu.com
               www.coachfederation.org

Things to remember

- Coaching is an essential business skill.
- Many managers do not possess the appropriate skills or do not use them as often as they should.
- Coaching is only part of the manager's role and should be used in balance with other skills.
- Managers should fully understand what coaching is and what it entails before using these skills.
- Coaching is not training, mentoring or counselling.

"A coach is someone who helps you hear what you don't want to hear, who helps you see what you don't want to see, in order that you can be who you have always known you could be."
Tom Landry – Former Coach for the Dallas Cowboys-U.S.A.

CHAPTER 2

Coaching Requisites and Pre-Suppositions

I hope that you have followed the previous chapter's suggested actions and as a result you are more aware of what coaching is and how it fits in with the other skills that a manager must possess in order to be successful.

"So, okay," you might be thinking, "I now know what coaching is and what it entails, but what do I have to do to put it into practice?"

Before you even attempt to coach, you need to think about the beliefs and pre-suppositions an effective coach has to have. Good, effective coaches presuppose and believe the following:

➤ Everyone lives in their own unique model or map of the world and people always make the best choice available to them, given their map and their perception of the situation.
➤ People cannot, not respond, therefore everything you say and do influences.
➤ The meaning of communication is the response it elicits. The intention behind a communication is not necessarily the same as it's meaning.
➤ All behaviour is motivated by a positive intention.

- There is no such thing as failure only feedback and everyone should have the chance to learn from mistakes.
- The person with the most behavioural flexibility in an interaction will have the greatest likelihood of achieving their outcome.
- Everyone already has all the resources (personal qualities) required to take the next step towards achieving his outcome.

In addition, there are some coaches who also believe these three things as well:

- A leader cannot lead without a following.
- The autocratic, power-based, boss faces extinction.
- The manager is there as a support, not as a threat.

As you look at some of these beliefs, think about what your beliefs are. My experience when I have discussed beliefs with managers has been mixed; with some wholeheartedly agreeing that they have similar beliefs and some who deny they think this way. The beliefs that cause the most debate are:

- All behaviour is motivated by a positive intention.
- There is no such thing as failure, only feedback.
- Everyone already has all the resources (personal qualities) required to take the next steps towards achieving their outcome.

Some managers make judgements regarding their staff, some of which are based on very little fact. They make assumptions such as these: "She is useless," "He is lazy," "They are not team players." There are many more, but what is particularly confusing is that these comments are usually made about people who have been recruited by the manager making the comments.

By having the positive beliefs outlined earlier as opposed to negative judgments, the manager is in a much better position to coach effectively. If an employee is not performing as well as expected, then the manager should look closely at what is causing this before making quick judgements about the employee or their actions.

Beliefs are important because they play such a vital role in the way a manager chooses to operate. A manager who believes that people cannot be trusted will never coach or manage effectively until he shifts that belief to one, which is more people-oriented. Think about what you really believe about people. Do you feel people can be trusted? Do you believe that your employees exist only to do as you say? Are your beliefs different outside of work? If so, why are they different and what is happening within the workplace that causes you to have different beliefs?

Working at this beliefs/values level is vital in order for effective coaching to take place. The manager must be aware of his own beliefs and values and must be prepared to share them with his peers and employees. How prepared are you to share?

A good coach or coaching manager will be able to help you discuss exactly what your beliefs are, and by doing so will begin to help you to raise your awareness about yourself and your beliefs. The greatest quality a manager can have is the quality of *awareness*. This is the product of focused attention, concentration, and clarity. While awareness includes both seeing and hearing, it is much more than that. Awareness considers feelings, gathering of relevant facts, and the ability to determine relevancy. This is accompanied by a good understanding of systems and processes, team dynamics, relationships, and some psychology. Awareness also includes the ability to realise one's own strengths and weaknesses.

In my years of experience, I discovered the degree of awareness each manager possessed varied considerably. While many were self-aware, realising their own strengths and weaknesses, the area of awareness that needed most attention was their understanding of how people and teams operated. Their knowledge of models and systems was very limited and that hindered their awareness, lessening their ability to coach effectively. How is your awareness? How would you rate your knowledge of team dynamics, team development models, and personality styles?

Once you have developed the skill of *awareness* of yourself and others, which also includes discernment of your beliefs and values, you will find that your level of *responsibility* rises. Next, you will be able to support the people you coach through this process. This will help them gain the confidence they need to accept responsibility for their actions. Telling does not produce responsibility. Coaching managers must coach their employees to help them make decisions and become accountable for them. We will look at how successful coaching managers can achieve this in a later chapter.

Following is a list of qualities of an effective coach. If you are not already, by the time you finish reading *The Successful Coaching Manager*, you will be familiar with all of these qualities.

- Self-Awareness
- Responsible
- Awareness
- Excellent Listener
- Patience
- Detached
- Supportive
- Interested
- Perceptive
- Attentive

➤   Retentive
➤   Able to challenge assumptions and actions
➤   Able to give and receive feedback

How do you rate on each of these qualities? What areas do you have to work on? You might want to ask for feedback from some of your colleagues to help raise your own awareness.

I have worked with, and met a few other managers who do not rate very highly on any of these qualities. They do not listen effectively, and they have low patience thresholds. They cannot remain detached since they feel they know the answers and because of this attitude, they cannot support the employees' concerns and ideas. They are not interested in learning to do it either, because they have other things to do. They lack concern for what is actually happening because they are preoccupied with these "other things."

Some managers have the capability to be good coaches, but their lack of time and personal management style does not allow them to be. Some just do not have the people skills to be effective coaches, and still others do not have the correct beliefs about people to coach successfully.

Am I painting a pretty poor picture of management? I believe that there is scope for great improvement in how managers operate and coach. I also believe that every manager has the potential to become a great coach within their management role provided they stop to reflect, get feedback from peers, and start to build their awareness to learn about their strengths and weaknesses. With the resultant feedback they should be able to build a personal development plan that will help to build their capabilities. Once managers realise that good coaching can bring more productivity for their staff and ultimately for themselves, they will rarely return to their old ways – unless stress gets to them. There is more about stress and its impact later in this book.

The challenge for all managers then, is to ensure that *awareness* and *responsibility* are developed in them and in their staff. A successful coaching manager will support this. Does your organisation have people who can coach effectively to raise individuals' awareness of their strengths and weaknesses? If not, act quickly!

Check your beliefs about people then compare them with the attitudes and beliefs of a good coach. Look at your own strengths and weaknesses and raise your *awareness* and your *responsibility*. Build a personal development plan, particularly in the area of coaching.

Now that you have raised your awareness of yourself and others and you are ready to take responsibility for your actions it is time to make an agreement with yourself and the people you want to coach. The next chapter will tell you how to contract.

CHAPTER 3

Contracting

Contracting is an essential skill not only for specialist coaches, but also for all managers. It is an important skill for the manager who has to deal with employees and knowing how to contract effectively can produce quick rapport and trust and prevent misunderstanding and conflict. I used to contract badly, if at all, and as a result, my ability to manage expectations and influence people suffered. Contracting in coaching is of utmost importance and time must be scheduled for it to happen effectively.

What is Contracting?

Contracting is simply, an agreement. Contracting is ensuring that all interested parties know specifically what is happening between individuals, and what that potentially means for them as individuals. Contracting is essential when building trust between a coach and the person being coached. It is extremely important for specialised coaches working either inside organisations or as external freelance coaches. The manager who coaches does not have to contract coaching with his respondents as fully as perhaps a specialist coach would, but a contract or "way of working" should be discussed in either case, covering all aspects of the manager's role. How routinely does this

14

happen? Not a lot in my experience.

Here are two examples to show how contracting works:

1. A new manager is meeting with an employee for the first time. An informal contract covering their working relationship might include questions like these:

   a. What motivates and de-motivates each of them?
   b. What are the expectations of the manager and the employee?
   c. What are the strengths and development areas of both the manager and the employee?
   d. How often and in what setting will review meetings take place?
   e. What structure does a regular review meeting have?

2. A specialist coach's contracting discussion will include the following in reference to coaching:

   a. How will the coaching session be instituted, for example, will it take place by telephone, face to face, or e-mail?
   b. What will the frequency and duration of coaching sessions be?
   c. What is the coach's style?
   d. It is important to discuss confidentiality. What is and is not privileged information?
   e. There must be feedback to determine when coaching is and is not being effective.

My belief is, if managers are successful in building an initial contract between themselves and employees they can also build a closer more trusting informal contract. It must though, be two-way for contracting to work effectively.

Contracting builds trust that will make it easier for a manager and an employee to work together. For specialised coaches, a contract would provide guidelines for working together, and in addition to that it would include specific aspects of coaching and confidentiality.

The confidentiality aspect of contracting can be incredibly stressful for internal company coaches in particular, but also for managers. Often senior managers will want to know details that affect an employee's performance and in some cases the coach and manager may be asked or ordered to release details of conversations. The coach or manager can then end up in the middle, risking a breach of contract with the employee as well as experiencing the wrath of the senior manager when it is looked upon as withholding information. Being able to manage or influence upwards is vital. This is another example of where contracting is very important. Contracting is about managing peoples' expectations whether they are a new recruit, employee of longevity, or the chief executive.

As a manager, you contracted with your employee to influence your working relationship, and you may have included within that discussion, details of how you would like to use the skill of coaching to help the employee develop and be successful. Within management, coaching can happen in two main ways:

1.   **Performance Coaching (on the job)**
       An example of this could be observing a sales representative's presentation and the manager/coach reviewing the sales call. Coaching in this instance would provide support for the sales representative to identify the strong and weak points of the

presentation. Questions used to evaluate it could be similar to these: "Which parts of it were effective and which parts were not so effective"? "How was the representative feeling before, during, and after the presentation"? "What kinds of observations did the sales person make about the customer" "What would be done differently next time?"

2. **Dedicated Time Coaching**

This type of coaching takes place within a certain time frame, an hour time slot, for example, and specific topics are identified and discussed. Following are some examples of useful questions: "How can I build my development plan"? "I'm struggling with Objective Number 2. How can I get back on track?" "How can I influence that major customer to buy my products?"

Discussions with managers confirm that a lot of good performance coaching occurs while "on the job." Most managers I have worked with agree that Dedicated Time Coaching does not happen to the degree it should. There are "review" meetings held but too often they are intended for the employee to keep the manager up to date with their progress, and for the manager to report the outcomes to someone more senior.

This is where the individual manager has to look at personal management skills. Managers must build both aspects of coaching into their schedules since effective coaching utilises the two elements in combination to build both capability and performance in the individual. All managers should be coached in personal management. Think about these awareness-evoking questions. How would you answer them? "How do you structure your day?" "How would you describe the balance between performance coaching and dedicated time coaching?"

"How much coaching time do you manage to build in?"

I am not going to start a discussion of time management techniques in this space; there are numerous books on the subject. It is, however, vitally important that managers organise and manage themselves effectively if effective coaching is going happen.

As a manager, contract how you and your employee will work together. The contract should include time for coaching. If you are a specialised coach add provisions for confidentiality and trust. Make sure that you contract with all your relevant "stakeholders." Trust comes from managing expectations and keeping the contract.

Once the contract is established, plan time to start coaching, and create a balance between Performance Coaching and Dedicated Time Coaching. If you are struggling with the number of tasks that you have to perform as a manager then look at ways to use your time more wisely and develop personal management skills. Schedule time for your employees to discuss issues with you and coach them through their objectives, issues and dreams. This serves a dual purpose: it helps them to move forward as individuals and helps the company be more successful as well.

Contracting will be easier if you take time to build rapport with the person you are working with. The next chapter will clarify rapport by definition and show coaches the basics of accomplishing it.

CHAPTER 4

Building Rapport

Building rapport is essential if you are going to influence people and start the process of building trust. As mentioned earlier, trust is a vital component if the manager is going to coach effectively. You can quickly build rapport or a harmonic relationship with people if you follow some simple guidelines.

This chapter will give you greater understanding of behavioural or personality styles and suggest ways you can flex your own style to build rapport with your employees and your team. Flexing one's style can, under certain conditions, be difficult and tiresome, for example, in the case of dealing with stress. It is vital though that a manager leads the way and maintains rapport with employees at all times. I have seen too many managers refuse to change their style because their ego tells them that the employees should be flexing towards their style since they are the boss. The result is usually a "personality clash" and perhaps you can guess who stands to lose the most in that situation. However, if employees have the same knowledge of behavioural styles as the manager does, they can learn to flex and accommodate too, especially with their own team, colleagues, and customers. This will make it easier for everyone involved.

What are these behavioural styles, how do you identify them, and how do you adapt your style to theirs? There are numerous models of behavioural styles and they are all based on work done in the 1920's by the psychologist, Carl Jung. It would be beneficial for you to read more about his work as well as familiarise yourself with models, such as: Myers-Briggs Type Inventory (MBTI) and The Disc Personality Type – (Dominant, Influencing, Steady, Cautious) – DISC.

The Four Behavioural Styles

There has been a lot of research on behavioural style, producing many models, but they are all very similar. The model I will introduce you to was developed by Wilson Learning in the United States (*www.wilson-learning.com*). It is the one I have used most in my career, and I find it works well. I also like the work of Dr Michael Lillibridge entitled The People Map because it uses up-to-date and corporate language.

Both the Wilson Learning and Lillibridge models suggest that there are four distinct behavioural types. For each of us, our behavioural style can be viewed as our personal comfort zone, or the style we adopt most naturally when not under stress.

Labels are used to identify these four behavioural styles, however, they are only labels. It is most important to be aware of the characteristics of each, and not the definition of the word itself. It is also important to note there will be some crossover, in almost everyone; therefore there are no absolutes. Some characteristics will be far more prominent in some people's normal behaviour than in others.

Driver, Controlling, or Leader Style

People who fit into this category are business-like and formal in appearance. Their main priority is the task at hand, and the results achieved. Their pace is fast and decisive. They prefer an atmosphere in which they can control people and processes, and achieve acceptance through their productivity and competitiveness.

Drivers like to be in charge, seek productivity, and dislike loss of control. They want you to get to the point, because they are irritated by inefficiency and indecision. They measure their personal worth by the results they achieve, and their track record. Under pressure these people will assert themselves strongly, and dictate the way things are going to be; they are autocratic.

To influence and work with these people, support their goals and objectives, and demonstrate what your ideas will do, when you will do it, and the cost. They want results.

Analytical, Processing, or Task Style

People using this style appear somewhat formal and conservative. Their main priority is the job at hand, and the process needed to achieve it. Their pace is measured and systematic. They prefer an atmosphere that encourages careful preparation and achieves acceptance through being correct, logical, and thorough.

Analyticals want recognition for being correct, seek accuracy, and dislike embarrassment. They want you to be precise in your dealings with them, because they are irritated by unpredictability and surprises. They measure their personal worth by their degree of precision, accuracy, and activity.

Under pressure, these people will withdraw into their own world, and avoid contact with causes of stress.

To influence and work with this personality, you need to support their thinking, and show how your ideas will support their personal credibility.

People, Amiable, or Supporting Style

People Style individuals appear to be casual, but conforming. Their pace is slow and easy. They prefer to maintain relationships and avoid confrontation. Therefore, they prefer an atmosphere that encourages close relationships, and achieve acceptance through conformity and loyalty.

They need to be appreciated, seek attention, and try to avoid confrontation. They want to be pleasant because they are irritated by insensitivity and impatience. They measure their personal worth by their degree of compatibility with others, and the depth of their relationships.

Under pressure, people who have this behavioural style will submit or acquiesce.

In order to influence and work with them, their managers need to support their feelings, and show how their ideas will support their personal circumstances.

Free Spirit, Expressive, or Enthusing Style

Free Spirit style personalities appear to be more flamboyant. They have a tendency to interact within relationships and they dislike any loss of prestige. Their pace is fast and spontaneous. They try to create an atmosphere that encourages flexibility. They achieve acceptance through sociability and creating a stimulating environment.

They want to be admired, seek recognition, and dislike being ignored. They want you to be stimulating because they are irritated by routine and boredom. They measure their personal worth by the amount of recognition and acknowledgement (or complaints) they receive.

Under pressure, a free style behavioural type person will become offensive or sarcastic.

Managers who want to be successful influencing and working with a person who uses this style will need to support their dreams and ideas, and show how they can help enhance their standing with others.

Table 1 provides a quick reference for identifying these styles using body language.

Tips for Building Rapport with Driver, Controlling, or Leadership Style

Avoid:

- Wasting their time
- Being vague and rambling
- Getting too personal or try to get too close
- Being disorganised
- Straying from the purpose of the discussion
- Asking irrelevant questions
- Making wild claims
- Trying to control the call
- Trying to chitchat at length

Table 1 Body Language of Behavioural Styles

Behavioural Style Body Language	Driver, Controlling, Leadership Style	Analytical, Processing, or Task Style	People, Amiable, or Supporting Style	Free Spirit, Expressive, or Enthusing Style
Facial Expression	Fixed	Fixed	Varied	Varied
Eye Contact	Intense Long Duration	Reflective	Empathetic	Intense Short Duration, Scattered
Posture	Formal	Formal	Informal	Informal
Body Movement	Limited	Limited	More Mobility	More Mobility
Gestures *Size* *Frequency*	Small High	Small Low	Larger Low	Larger High
Voice Tone	Monotone	Monotone	Inflexion	Inflexion
Speed	Fast, Clipped	Slow, Measured	Slow, Measured	Fast
Volume/Force	Louder	Softer	Softer	Louder
Decision Making	Quick Limited Facts	Slower Lots of facts	Slower Lots of Opinions	Fast Intuition

Try to achieve:

- Getting down to business quickly
- Being specific in questioning
- Efficient time use
- Providing alternatives for them to choose from
- Being factual and succinct
- Talking about results and outcomes
- Avoiding too much detail

Tips for Building Rapport with Analytical, Processing, or Task Style

Avoid:

- Being disorganised and casual
- Being late
- Providing personal incentives
- Pushing or coaxing
- Using testimonials or options
- Being flippant or gimmicky

Try to achieve:

- Being well prepared
- Getting straight down to business
- Listening carefully
- Being specific and logical
- Being persistent and thorough when questioning
- Being formal and unemotional when challenging
- Giving them time to put in their point of view

Tips for building rapport with People, Amiable, or Supporting Style

Avoid:

- Going straight into your discussion
- Keeping the discussion subject focused all the time
- Causing them to respond quickly
- Dominating or controlling the discussion
- Being rapid or abrupt
- Keeping offering opinions or increasing the complexity of the decision
- Making wild claims
- Being very factual

Try to achieve:

- Being friendly to show an interest in them personally
- Being prepared for some chitchat before getting down to business
- Taking time to uncover their needs by asking open questions
- Being alert for non-verbal cues of dissatisfaction or disagreement
- Being informal
- Presenting your facts and points in a non-threatening way
- Including guarantees and assurances wherever possible
- Giving your presentation the personal touch

Tips for Building Rapport with Free Spirit, Expressive, or Enthusing Style

Avoid:

➤ Controlling the discussion and keeping strictly to business

➤ Being impatient

➤ Inputting too much detail into the presentation

➤ Tying them down there and then in making decisions

➤ Socialising too much

➤ Patronising or digging your heels in

Try to achieve:

➤ Some element of socialising before the business

➤ Talking about opinions and other people

➤ Outline your ideas about what is being discussed

➤ Being enthusiastic and energetic

➤ Being fast paced

➤ Offering incentives

It is vital for the manager who wants to coach effectively to become skilled at building rapport quickly and easily. Knowing your own style and the styles of the people you manage, can help you to build rapport by "leading the way" and flexing your style.

The next chapter introduces the GROW and OUTCOMES™ models of coaching which will show us how to put this theory into practice.

CHAPTER 5

Using the GROW and OUTCOMES™ Models

The first few chapters of this book have been aimed at preparing the manager to be in a position to start to coach. I have talked about learning more about what specifically coaching is and skills that coaches need. These include mindsets, beliefs and values. Contracting is an essential skill for specialist coaching as well as for coaching managers to create a clear picture of expectations and develop trust. Identifying behavioural styles will help in building rapport.

You can use a simple coaching model called GROW to get you started using coaching skills to support development in yourself and the people you manage. The GROW model is defined in Sir John Whitmore's *Coaching for Performance*.

In this model the acronym GROW is delineated by letters that symbolise each part of it.

G - GOAL

R - REALITY

O - OPTIONS

W- WRAP UP and/or WILL. (I will expand on this a bit later.)

We will look at each part of the model, but before we do, here is a *health warning*!

This coaching model works well if it is used appropriately and the manager or coach does not use the framework as just a means of asking a few questions. For example, I have heard of managers asking one or two questions per section:

> What is your goal? What do you want to achieve?
>
> Where are you now? What is the gap?
>
> What options do you have to fill the gap?
>
> When are you going to do the things you need to do?

FINISH. Quick coaching session. But no real depth was reached and no exploration was used to determine what is really happening with the coached person. The secret of using GROW is to explore and to support the coached person by specifically finding out what they really want to achieve. This helps to ensure they fully understand where they are right now and to assess the reality of their goals. Time must be taken to go through all the options available, to test the validity of each option and to test which option is the best choice.

Finally, rather than just "WRAP UP" as the GROW model suggests, the "WILL" of the coached person to carry out the actions needed must be tested and confirmed. There is no point in identifying what the specific goal is, and exploring all the options to find a way forward, and then finding the necessary motivation to perform the actions does not exist.

Using GROW should take time. GROW is not intended to answer only a few quick questions. That is not what true coaching is. Managers must be prepared to spend time to ensure, what I call "dedicated time coaching." Helping people move through the GROW model slowly will be more effective. Rushing through could preclude the best results and or result in total de-motivation.

This is how we can make the GROW model really work for the manager and those being coached. Invest the time, at least an hour or more depending on the topic being discussed.

G – GOAL

Set goals. Take time to fully explore exactly what they are trying to achieve. Check the realism of their goals. If what they are trying to achieve is beyond their capabilities, or not within budgets, then help them to rethink and choose a more realistic target. You may have to work hard on this one to continue to motivate the individual and perhaps set a longer term to accomplish their dreams. Make sure their objectives are SMART.

You must help them set Specific, Measurable, Achievable, Realistic, and Time-bound goals, but overall make sure they are "stretching." Coaching is about action, success, and growth, so objectives must be challenging, but not so challenging that they are not achievable.

R – REALITY

Is the goal realistic? Check exactly where the coached person is currently in relation to goals or objectives. Be prepared to challenge and give feedback where necessary. I have worked with some people whose grasp of reality in relation to where they are objectively is undetermined. Some people actually need to be told they are not as prepared as they think they are. Other people are actually further ahead than they think they are. The issue is not to tell them outright where specifically they are but to enable them to realize that for themselves. Feedback is helpful in this instance. We will look at giving and receiving feedback later in this book.

O – OPTIONS

What are their choices? Don't settle for the first option that comes into the person's head. Explore, explore, explore. Support that person to come up with a few options and then test each option by taking time to investigate the pros and cons of each. Get him to make a decision - a personal decision - about what is best. I emphasise it must be a personal decision because this is an area where managers can manipulate people. A manager might decide which choice is best, and then "lead" the person to thinking this option is the best choice.

Managers have to take risks and let the employees choose for themselves. If the manager manipulates the person to do his bidding, then where will the motivation to carry out that option come from? This is the area where I have seen potentially good coaching managers fall down. They explore and identify the goals well, they support their people to investigate the options, and then they manipulate to get the person to carry out the option the manager is most comfortable with. Don't do it - take a risk. I have been coached in this way on occasion and, believe me, it is not the best way.

W – WRAP UP and/or WILL

Some books call the process of summarising all of this WRAP-UP. It involves reinforcing the goal or objective, planning the steps necessary to achieve that goal and setting the time period in which to achieve each step. I prefer to call it WILL since I believe that you can WRAP-UP and go, but, perhaps, the coached person does not feel fully motivated or capable of carrying out the actions. You must check this and you must have the awareness to identify if the motivation is really what it should be.

Be aware of body language, and voice tone. Is it synergistic with the other steps? Ask them to tell you on a scale of 1–10, how motivated they are to carry out the necessary steps they have agreed on. Use number 1 to designate "not motivated at all", and number 10 to show "really buzzing, can't wait to get started". Be prepared to challenge them if you see the smallest hint of a lack of motivation.

You can now go out and try to use GROW. Remember to contract with your people. Also, keep reading and enlist the support of your mentor or coach. Some coaches may have different ideas from the ones you are seeing here. The more information, advice, and practice you get the better.

The OUTCOMES™ Coaching System

Personally, I feel that many managers do not use the traditional GROW model as well as they should. They do not spend as much time as perhaps they should at each of the stages and as such do not explore realities of situations and the options available in as much depth as they should. I believe that a more structured model with extra steps would help them achieve this depth. To support this I have developed the OUTCOMES™ Coaching System. Let me take you through it.

O = Objectives
It is important for a manager to assist their employee identify their objectives, either for their overall role or for a particular situation be it a sales call or simply for a specific coaching session. Taking time to support the employee discover their objectives is vital and once this is achieved and the "fog" lifted you can see a visible improvement in an employee's morale. Many employees simply do not understand what they have to specifically achieve in their roles and as such become de-motivated.

U = Understand the Reasons
The second stage is to ensure that both the manager and the employ-

ee understand what the exact reasons are behind the objectives. For what purpose do they want to achieve a particular objective? Sometimes employees want to achieve something in particular without thinking through whether it is a priority or not. It is estimated that 90% of managers spend their time working on non-priority areas and as such are not as productive as they could be. One of the reasons behind this was that they were trying to achieve objectives that they felt they had to be seen to be achieving by senior management. The reality was this was not what senior management wanted to see!

So, by getting to understand the exact reasons why people are trying to achieve a particular objective, the manager can assist the employee to analyse what they are trying to achieve and why. In my experience, many original aims of employees "go out the window" and they re-assess what they actually should be aiming to achieve.

T= Take Stock of the Present Situation

It is important to take time and analyse exactly where an employee is in relation to a particular objective. How much have they achieved so far? Are they starting from "zero" or have they gone some way to achieving it already? Once a "reality check" has been performed, then you are in a position to move forward.

C = Clarify the Gap

Once you have "Taken Stock" of the present situation then it is important to clarify exactly what the gap is between where the employee is now in relation to the objective and what they still have to do to achieve the objective's outcomes. Again this stage takes time.

O = Options Analysis

Once the actual gap is clear in the employee's mind in relation to what they have to do, then it is the manager's role as coach to assist them to identify how best they can "close the gap" and achieve the objective. Too often, managers accept the first option and many cases the employee comes up with what he or she thinks the manager wants to hear! This results in usually the same old behaviours and "tried and trusted" methods.

The employee must be allowed to explore all the options available in terms of the pros and cons of each. Only this way will you get a best option available for that particular employee. This is the way that new methods are encountered and as a result the employee and the company can grow

M = Motivate to Action

If the manager has taken time over the previous stages then at this point the employee will have a way forward that they themselves have come up with and as a result they should be motivated to move forward the actions that are necessary. Make sure that they write down these actions and the manager should do likewise.

Watch out for any physical signs of a lack of motivation. Many managers do not take time over the previous stages and "lead" (or manipulate) the employee through the coaching process with a view to ensuring that the employee comes up with the manager's idea of what the employee should do. This should be avoided at all costs as it only leaves the employee de-motivated and this should show. Be aware of body language and voice tone and if you have any inkling that the employee is not motivated to carry out the actions that they have outlined then challenge them supportively to find out why.

E = Encourage and Enthuse

Managers do not do enough of this! I have put this stage in because I have seen many managers "leave" the coaching process once the employee has a set of actions after going through the coaching process. Although they seem motivated the employee needs that motivation reinforced and what better way to do it through a bit of praise. Tell them, "well done" for coming up with the actions and thanks them for their time in going through the coaching process. A small bit of praise can work wonders!

S = Support

The final stage is about what support the employee needs from the manager in order to continue to be motivated to carry out the actions discussed. This doesn't mean doing the actions for the employee but could mean, perhaps, a weekly or even monthly progress check, or simply having an "open door" or "open phone" policy whereby the employee can access advice or simply share success. Support coaching by phone can be very effective and very few managers employ this skill.

The OUTCOMES™ coaching system, I believe, will enable managers (when trained effectively) to coach their employees in a more structured and effective way than perhaps they are presently used to doing. Whilst GROW will remain the standard coaching model for generic coaching, OUTCOMES™ will be a really useful addition to the manager's coaching armoury

The next chapter will address listening, a skill that is paramount to using the GROW and OUTCOMES™ models effectively, as well as developing the skills of "great coach."

CHAPTER 6

Listening

Listening is probably the most under-used skill that managers possess. There is so much going on in a manager's mind - performance issues, discipline issues, budgets, appointments, customers, you name it – that sometimes putting all this in the background temporarily can be difficult.

Zeno of Citium, founder of the Stoic school of philosophy said: "The reason we have two ears and only one mouth is that we may listen the more and talk the less."

What is Listening Exactly, and Why is it so Important in Coaching?

Listening is a process of absorbing words and selecting meanings. It is a skill, and can therefore be developed and improved. Self-awareness and discipline are needed in order to be a good listener to convince the speaker that you are listening, hence attempting to really understand what is being said. This is why it is so vital in coaching. The coach needs to listen in order to really understand how the coached person feels. When a coached person sees and feels that they are being listened to, trust and openness begin to build and true coaching can take place.

Do you remember the last time you were telling somebody something and you got that feeling that you weren't being listened to? Were you interrupted? Did you have to repeat what you said? Did you see their eyes wander when another person entered the room? How did you feel when this happened?

There are certain cues that you can give to speakers to let them know you are listening and paying attention. You can nod, or ask questions to clarify what they said. Repeating back to them what they said to confirm that you heard them correctly is another way to show the speaker you are listening. When asking questions for clarification, choose words carefully to show that it is clarification you are seeking and not that you were not listening. Most people listen at about 50% efficiency during the first part of a conversation and this can quickly deteriorate to 25% overall. But, if you are a manager who wants to coach effectively, how can you raise that percentage closer to 100%?

Before a conversation or coaching session begins make sure:

➤ You have time and you are not in a hurry. If you have been hurried, calm down and compose yourself. Manage your time when coaching.

➤ You empty your mind as best you can - you are there for the person you are coaching in mind and body.

➤ You won't be distracted by what is going on around you.

➤ Don't be bored! You are the coach; you must treat everyone with respect. (Remember the section about beliefs and values?)

➤ You try not to think about what you are going to say next.

➤ You do not let models like GROW dictate how you

proceed. Use them accordingly.

➤ You don't guess what the other person is going to say next.

➤ You don't go in with hidden agendas - don't manipulate.

➤ If you are tired, you will consider rescheduling.

➤ You focus on enjoying the coaching session.

There Are Three Kinds of Listeners:

1. *Passive Listeners* are those who appear to be listening but do not really digest fully all that you are saying.

2. *Non-Responsive Listeners* are those who give very little indication as to whether or not they are fully listening.

3. *ActiveListeners* are those who interact in a two-way conversation or exchange and through their attentiveness reassure you that they are listening fully.

Active listening is the best of the three choices. To be a successful active listener, it is best to listen not only to the words but also to the intentions behind the words, to look at the speaker's body language and to listen to non-verbal cues, such as these:

➤ Convey a positive, encouraging attitude

➤ Sit in an attentive posture – don't slouch.

➤ Remain alert but comfortable

➤ Nod in acknowledgement

➤ Make eye contact or match (remember not to mimic) eye contact

➤ Ignore or eliminate distractions

> ➤ Tune in to the speaker's feelings
> ➤ Look like a listener!
> ➤ Don't fidget, play with rings, or hair
> ➤ Don't, for goodness' sake, look at your watch!
> ➤ Don't use the coaching session as a chance to sit down and have a breather – listening is tough, but very rewarding work

I remember a senior manager asking me why I looked tired. I had performed three coaching sessions that day, and each person I coached had a different style from my own. First, I had to adapt my style (tiring, but rewarding), then I had to listen intently (tiring, but rewarding) and finally I had to coach them through some issues and goals (tiring, but rewarding). I *was* tired, but happy that I had supported these people to motivate them. The manager could not believe that, as he saw it, "sitting down and chatting with people" was not tiring. If you are not tired after a coaching session, but happy, then you haven't been coaching.

What about Taking Notes?

Notes can be a memory-jogger for later use and a distraction. Taking notes can interfere with listening and put you one step behind the speaker. If you want to take notes during a session, then do it in some form of shorthand. I use mind maps, which are best described as a "flow" of "doodles." You can see this at (*http://www.buzancentre.com*). I find it helps me maintain eye contact and keep track of the conversation. They are also useful for reviewing the issues or goals when planning the next coaching session.

Oh, one last thing, *turn off your mobile phone.* If you are going to coach then turn your attention to the person you are coaching. Forget about the "I'm waiting for an important phone call" nonsense.

If you are going to be a successful coaching manager then you must give your employees the attention they deserve. You must learn to listen and understand your people, to coach them to greater things. One reason for listening is so we can give and receive feedback, which helps us become aware of how our behaviour affects others.

CHAPTER 7

Giving and Receiving Feedback

The last chapter was dedicated to a skill that is vital for managers who want to coach, effectively: listening. The ability to give and receive quality feedback is another vital skill for managers. This is an important tool, which can be used to heighten the awareness of the manager and employee. Remember awareness is also a vital component of being an effective coach.

How many of you who are reading this consider yourself to be good at giving and receiving feedback? How do you feel when someone gives you feedback that perhaps you don't want to hear? Do you "switch off" thinking if you are going to respond it will be only to defend yourself? Or worse, do you interrupt with the magical, "*But . . .*"? Do you avoid offering someone constructive feedback (sometimes called negative or developmental) because you either are not aware of the reaction you might get, or because you know the reaction will be negative?

Most of us are good at giving praise – well, those of us who give it regularly are, and giving praise is not just a nice to do, it is an essential thing to do. We all like to receive praise as well. Giving feedback that challenges people's behaviour is quite different. If it is given in the wrong way some people's reaction when receiving it can be, to say the least, disturbing.

I like to think of myself as someone who is able to give both praise and constructive feedback. However, there are still some people who I really struggle with, either because their reaction is defensive, or worse, they nod, agree to change, and then go away from the discussion, discount the feedback, and continue their old ways. Perhaps it is the way I deliver the feedback to these people that makes it difficult, or even impossible for them to use it constructively.

If you are going to be a successful coaching manager then you have to develop the ability to give feedback as well as receive it yourself. I have seen too many managers talk behind people's backs, or worse still, share concerns about team members with other members. Instead of getting issues out in the open, where individuals can do something about them, discussions go on behind "closed doors" and issues start to become exaggerated. Getting the issues out in the open clears the air, and gives people a chance to improve their situations. Giving and receiving feedback is one of the most important motivational tools a manager or coach can have.

Feedback should be used to:

➤   Enhance performance
➤   Aid problem solving
➤   Assist in helping us to see our blind spots
➤   Provide a way of learning more about ourselves and
          the effect our behaviour has on others
➤   Develop self-awareness
➤   Reward and provide recognition
➤   Motivate
➤   Say "Thank you"

These are some of the implications of not using feedback:

➢ Less chance of behavioural change - maintains status quo

➢ Other person may be unaware of deficiencies (which could be damaging to them and others)

➢ May eventually become a confrontation

➢ Less opportunity for other person to learn and develop

➢ They may not recognise *your* achievements / successes

➢ They may not *thank you*!!

There are three different types of feedback: Praise, Constructive Criticism, and Three-Part Assertion Messages.

1. **Praise** is used when someone has met or exceeded your expectations. It can be expressed in ways similar to these:

    ➢ Give specific examples ("Thanks for passing on that information about ...")

    ➢ Mention the personal qualities that you think the person displayed ("It showed a real willingness to share information and be supportive when you . ..")

    ➢ Mention the resulting benefit to you / the team / the business ("As a result of your . . . I was able to go in to see him before he had decided...")

2. **Constructive Criticism** is used when you trying to change behaviour. Give balanced feedback by:

> Specifying the merits you want retained ("The way you kicked that ball was brilliant, hard and straight.")

> Specify the concerns you want eliminated ("I'm a bit worried though about how close it went to Mr. Smart's patio windows.")

> Explore ideas / solutions together ("Let's see if we can figure out a way together to keep the ball away from his patio.")

or

> "You really managed to get an excellent turn-out at the meeting, although the speaker didn't help us by what he said about our product. Why don't we work on some ideas together so we get a much more positive endorsement at future meetings?"

3.   **Three Part Assertion Messages** can be used when situations such as, the following are occur-ring:

> There is potential for the person to modify/change their behaviour.

> There is a low probability that you will violate their personal space and/or diminish their self-esteem (e.g., it is totally inappropriate to give people feedback which is likely or designed to de-motivate or embarrass some one.)

> There is low risk of damaging the relationship between you.

> There is low risk of inducing defensiveness.

These are some examples of how to use them:

> Describe the defending behaviour non-judgemen-tally (You raised your voice when you started speak-ing" *not* "You shouted at me / you were angry at me."

> Disclose your feelings (". . . and that made me feel frightened / angry / confused / disappointed.")

> Describe the consequence of the behaviour ("because I didn't know what you were going to do next and that's making it difficult for me to concen-trate on the task at hand.")

Giving and receiving feedback sometimes takes "guts." It is, though, a vital skill for managers, coaches, and indeed for anyone who wants to develop better communication skills. I have seen great shifts in peo-ple's skills and motivations when they learn to give and receive feed-back. I have also seen, and still see, the opposite where people do not have the courage or ability to give and receive feedback. These people are "stuck!"

Some people remain "stuck," and consequently make mistakes. Some learn from their mistakes. The next chapter lists common coaching mistakes and ideas you can use to avoid making them.

CHAPTER 8

Some Common Coaching Mistakes

These are the "top ten" coaching mistakes that managers and coaches can make. They can have a lasting negative effect on both managers and their employees, so beware!

MISTAKE 1 You don't invest the time

In order for coaching to happen, you have to schedule time for it. It doesn't always take dedicated time to coach. It can be done "on the job," called performance coaching, and it may only last a few minutes. But you will need to set specific time aside for dedicated coaching, especially where you are really attempting to support your employees through particular issues that require deep understanding. If you are struggling with your workload then consider some time management techniques to help you manage it. Scheduling time for coaching your employees will bring untold benefits in the future.

MISTAKE 2 You forget to contract

Recently I asked a number of managers if they had contracted their roles with their employees. Almost all of them did not know what a contract was, and of those who did some did not know specifically what was involved in a contract. After I explained it, most of the managers admitted to assuming that their employees knew what was expected from the managers. Assumptions do not always reflect reality. A contract is essential so everyone who is involved will know and understand what the expectations are. A contract is the best way of managing expectations and developing a good working relationship. A firm contract is essential if you are a specialised coach.

MISTAKE 3 You break the contract

A contract is the beginning of building trust and respect, which are vitally important to any working relationship. Break the contract and you run the risk of the relationship breaking down, sometimes for good. The biggest source of broken contracts is confidentiality. If you are a "gossip merchant" then beware. Change your habits or suffer the consequences.

MISTAKE 4 You fail to build rapport

You need to know your own behavioural style and know how to identify other people's styles. You should be able to flex your own style to match others and thereby build rapport or harmony. Failure to build rapport can, like a broken contract, lead to non-productive working relationships.

MISTAKE 5 You use GROW inappropriately

The GROW model is an excellent coaching model but care must be taken to explore each of the stages. You must also be very flexible, since you may have to "jump about" through the model, revisiting goals, or checking on reality, as well as fully exploring every option. On a number of occasions I have gotten to the Wrap-Up or Will stage only to find that the Will is not there because the goals are unrealistic at that point in time. Do not use the model quickly - failure to explore fully will possibly lead to the wrong conclusions and actions and perhaps to frustration and de-motivation.

MISTAKE 6 You fail to listen intently

There is nothing worse than a poor listener, especially when someone is attempting to help you understand what is going on in her work or life. Not listening or allowing yourself to become distracted during a conversation can lead to great frustration on behalf of the listener. Find a quiet comfortable spot away from a lot of noise before you begin any coaching sessions. Find a quiet spot to coach and *turn the mobile telephone off*!

MISTAKE 7 You are manipulative in your questioning

One of the hardest things coaches or managers have to do is to "distance" themselves from the content of a conversation. In coaching you should not manipulate the employee into doing things that you would do, or doing them in a way that you would prefer. You have every right to think that a task should be done a particular way; you, however, do not have a right to impose it on the employee. Who can say that your way is the best way in the first place? Do not use your questions to lead the employee to your way of thinking. You might leave the coaching session satisfied that your employee is going to do your bidding, but you can bet that more often than not, the employee will not be motivated to carry out the actions.

MISTAKE 8 You do not take calculated risks

Taking calculated risks is a big challenge for managers under pressure. They ruminate over questions such as these. What if it goes wrong? What if senior managers find out that an employee did it their own way and not the way you would like them to do it? What would happen if they did it their way, and that way turned out to be the most productive way? Take the risks, and provided you have ensured the employee has the capability, rarely will you regret it. You may want, though, to be in a position to effectively manage your superiors.

MISTAKE 9 You coach when you shouldn't

Learn to distinguish between coaching and counselling. If sessions are beginning to get very "personal" and conversations become too "psychological" then prepare to back off and refer to a qualified counsellor. But it doesn't always have to be a "counselling" situation where you don't coach. There are other interventions that you have to use when helping people in developmental stages. These include: giving direction, guiding and delegating. The next chapter of *The Successful Coaching Manager* will explain the Capability / Motivation Grid which will help in this area.

MISTAKE 10 You do not ask for regular feedback

How do you know your coaching is effective? How well is the contract working? What is working well? What is not working well? Continually checking progress is essential for the coaching relationship to develop and become stronger. Finally, in relation to your feedback to your employees, remember to *praise* them for things they do well. *Praise is the most powerful form of feedback.* Many managers do not use enough appropriate praise.

Now that you know the most common coaching mistakes, don't make it common to make them yourself.

CHAPTER 9

Adopting the Appropriate Coaching Approach

In my early days as a manager, I was often surprised by the reaction I got when I either delegated a task or simply told someone what to do. The result: the task was not completed or was done in an incorrect manner. It was not until I spoke to people about the reasons why the work was not done or why it was not completed correctly, that I started to question myself, about what I should have done. Then I was introduced to Blanchard's Situational Leadership model and The Skill/Will Matrix or Capability / Motivation Grid, and it all started to make sense to me.

I was delegating tasks inappropriately, because I was delegating tasks to someone who was unwilling or unable to complete the job, therefore, I remained relatively hands-off or uninvolved. Alternatively, I may have been hands-on or directive with a capable person who was quite able to complete the assignment with little assistance from me; I just ended up frustrating them.

I also remember when I was being "coached" by a senior manager in a task that was new to me. They asked me all sorts of questions expecting me to come up with the answers and I became incredibly frustrated since I could not find the answers. What I really needed was someone to tell me the answers so I could at least get started on the task. Ever been there? Annoying isn't it?

Consequently, whether you are coaching or managing, it is critical to match your style of coaching interaction with the employee's readiness for the task.

The Skill/Will Matrix or the Capability / Motivation Grid will enable you to do this. The model is divided into four quadrants:

1. **LOW CAPABILITY / LOW MOTIVATION**
   The beginner in a role, project or task who is just starting out and is nervous or may have already tried and failed.

2. **HIGH MOTIVATION / LOW CAPABILITY**
   The enthusiastic beginner new to a particular role, project or task.

3. **LOW MOTIVATION / HIGH CAPABILITY**
   The skilled experienced person who is in need of attention and might be affected by the challenge of change.

4. **HIGH CAPABILITY / HIGH MOTIVATION**
   The skilled worker who is looking for more opportunities to grow and develop.

Using this Model

Step 1: Diagnose whether the coached person's skill and will are high or low, for the specific task to be accomplished. Remember that it is related to the specific task and not to overall experience. You may have someone who you think is High Motivation / High Capability overall because of their performances, but where are they on the grid if you give them a new task where their capabilities may not be evident?

- **Capability** – Skill depends on experience, training, understanding, and role perception.
- **Motivation** – Will depends on desire to achieve, incentives, security, and confidence.

Step 2: Identify the appropriate coaching/management style; for example, use Guide if the coachee has high motivation but low capability for the task.

	Low Capability	High Capability
High Motivation	Guide/Coach	Delegate/Support
Low Motivation	Direct/Instruct	Excite/Coach

Step 3: Agree on your intended approach with the person you are coaching.

Applying the Model

Direct / Instruct (capability and motivation are both low)
➤ First build the will / motivation:

- Provide clear and concise briefings
- Identify motivators and de-motivators
- Develop a vision of future performance
- Ensure understanding of requirements

➤ Then build the skill / capability:
  - Structure tasks for quick wins
  - Identify training requirements
  - Coach and train

➤ Finally the motivation:
  - Provide frequent feedback against progress
  - Praise and nurture

➤ Ensure close supervision with clear rules and deadlines.

Guide / Coach (low capability, high motivation)

➤ Invest time early to ensure inclusion and understanding of training requirements
  - Coach and Train
  - Answer questions/explain
➤ Create a risk-free environment to allow early mistakes/learning
➤ Monitor progress regularly and ensure feedback and praise
➤ Relax control as progress is shown

Excite / Coach (high capability, low motivation)

➤ Identify reasons for low motivation - (task/management style/personal factors)
➤ Motivate appropriately

➤   Monitor feed back
➤   Ensure scope for regular progress checks – evaluation.

Delegate / Support (capability and motivation are both high)
➤   Provide freedom to do the job
  •   Set objectives, not method
  •   Praise, don't ignore

➤   Encourage coachee to take responsibility
  •   Involve in decision-making
  •   Say, "You tell me what you think."

➤   Take appropriate risks
  •   Give more challenging tasks ensuring support in place
  •   Don't over-manage

Applying the capability / motivation principles will enable you to ensure that you are taking the appropriate approach with each individual in the team when you are asking them to perform tasks.

A "great coach," can be trusted to assess the abilities and interest levels of the people they coach. Trust is an important part of other facets of coaching too. Chapter 10 will expand on the importance of trust.

CHAPTER 10

The Importance of Trust

Trust is vital for coaches and managers if they want to enable people to be as effective and productive as they can be. Break someone's trust and you face an uphill battle in terms of supporting a person's development.

Here are ten strategies you can use to develop trust in a coaching relationship:

1. **Have Clear and Consistent Objectives**
    Be sure you know what you are trying to achieve with individuals and that they are in agreement with that. Don't tell them you would like to achieve one thing and then set your sights on another goal. If you do change the goals then tell your people. Keep them informed.

2. **Be Open, Fair, and Willing to Listen Intently**
    Be open and honest with people you coach. Share your feelings, hopes, and concerns, and show how these elements pertain to them. Treat all those you deal with fairly. Be consistent in your approach with everyone. Avoid having favourites. I have worked

with managers in the past who have had favourites. All that leads to is mistrust and broken working relationships. You cannot coach effectively when this happens.

Show a genuine interest in what the other person is saying by learning and practicing active empathetic listening skills. Set up ways of making yourself accessible to others; you might consider an open door policy.

3. **Be Decisive**

As a manager you must be decisive. Even a bad decision is better than no decision when it comes to building trust. As a coach you must be decisive, too. You expect people to be decisive when it comes to making decisions about the best way to move forward; lead by example.

4. **Support all the Team Members**

Earlier I mentioned the dangers of having favourites. As a coach you should treat all members of the team in a similar way. Obviously your individual approach to each member will vary slightly because of their behavioural styles and where they are in relation to the Capability/Motivation Grid but you should strive to treat them equally.

5. **Take Responsibility**

If you are a manager of a team and something goes wrong, what do you do? Point fingers? Don't! Take personal responsibility for the actions of the team as a whole. If someone makes a mistake, find the cause of that mistake and support whoever is involved to make certain it does not happen again.

I've seen too many managers abuse their position by "pointing the finger" and not accepting responsibility for the actions of the team. The classic example is the sales manager who blames certain members of the team for the team's sales results overall. Poor performance from some team members is usually due to poor leadership either through bad recruitment or an inability (capability or will) to develop and motivate the team members through leadership and coaching. There is nothing worse for a team than to see their manager not taking responsibility.

6. **Praise**

Praise is the most powerful form of feedback. Praise should be given when it is deserved. It should also be given in a sincere and non-superficial way. Doing it superficially, or worse, not at all, will kill, not cultivate trust. A coach or manager who does not praise is no coach.

I have seen some managers take the praise when it was actually belonged to another team member. Shocking! Do not take away another person's glory. As a coach, although your interventions may have enabled someone to succeed in a particular task, it was their physical actions that made it happen. Praise and congratulate them - they will realise who helped them achieve it.

7. **Try to Understand**

Learn to understand as much as you can about your

employees. When mistakes are made, do not jump to conclusions and brand them as "incompetent." Analyse what caused them to make the mistake and get to the root cause of issues. By listening and asking questions to uncover reasons for errors, you can build trust and people will become more open. Once you know the real reasons why a certain thing happens you can start to support them to rectify the situation. Start to blame immediately and trust vanishes. Successful coaching managers do not jump to quick conclusions.

8.   **Respect Opinions of Others**

You have your own opinions. Who are you to say that yours is right and someone else's is wrong? I listened to a manager recently say, "Look, I don't care what you say. I'm the boss." Will that build trust? Not likely.

Not everyone sees things the same way. That is not important. What is important is that everyone's opinion is listened to and respected. You may not agree and that is your choice. As a coach you must respect people's opinions. When you do, you will be amazed how many people change their opinions to mirror yours. If you do not respect them, you will never trust them. And they are not likely to trust you.

9.   **Encourage a "safe" Environment for Risk-Taking**

People need differing degrees of feeling safe before they take risks. Often in organisations, people are afraid to take risks because of the reputation of managers and their tendency to blame and look at mistakes as incompetence. The manager or coach should ensure that people feel safe in order for them to be empowered. Empower your people and watch them and the company grow. In my experience, empowerment failure results most of the time, because of the inability of managers to influence their senior managers.

10. **Keep Confidences**

There is nothing worse than breaking someone's confidence. If you are going to be a true coaching manager then you will find that as time goes on and you coach more effectively, people will begin to trust you more. You will be trusted with more confidential information. You must maintain these confidences within the terms of the contract that you have with your people. Break that contract by releasing confidential information and you break all the trust that has been built up. You may never recover. This is another area where I have seen managers fail badly. After gaining confidential information they break the contract by "gossiping" to other parties, perhaps the "favourites" in their team. Don't do it!

Whether you are a manager or a coach, trust is vital, for the relationship to succeed and grow. Remember we talked in an earlier chapter about contracting? If you contract right at the start of your coaching relationship, and, if you maintain the agreements within that contract then trust will blossom.

Add these ten strategies to your list of coaching skills, and you will have the basis for a fantastic and productive working relationship.

By now you are likely to agree that trust is paramount to a great coaching relationship. Sometimes there are things in the way that keep people from trusting. These are called blocks and barriers and the next chapter will not only list them, but help us find ways to overcome them.

CHAPTER 11

Blocks and Barriers

A block or a barrier to coaching is simply what it implies: something that prevents coaching from happening in the first place. There are a number of blocks and barriers. Some of them are listed below with suggestions to help you overcome them.

The Organisation and Senior Management

It may be that the organisation you work in has a "command and control" culture where the "boss is king" and what he or she says, goes. There can be great pressures on managers, who want to coach and take the time to coach, but senior managers can want things done now and they want them done their way. You may appear to be different and that can be taken the wrong way, so managers who want to coach must be strong enough to manage in such a way that senior management is aware of what is being done and why. You will have to influence and convince them so they can see it works. Be responsible for the results. Persuade them that using the coaching approach will increase results and productivity.

In general, those managers who prefer to operate in a "command and control" manner do so out of insecurity so you will need to reassure them that taking a coaching approach is not a risk for them and that results will follow.

Stand up for yourself, guarantee results, and keep senior management informed of progress, in areas such as increased productivity, morale, and capability. Show specifically how and why coaching was responsible for this.

Your Management Peers

Most of the managers I have worked with over the years have attempted to build their coaching capability. Some, however, have not for a variety of reasons. There are many reasons, but they all link to basic fear and insecurity. Some of these are listed below:

- ➤ Fear of authority: Scared that the boss will not agree. "I must follow the boss."
- ➤ Fear of the skills of coaching: "I might not be able to do it, and how will that look to the boss and my employees?"
- ➤ Fear of having something else to do: "I can't fit it in to my daily schedule because my time management is very poor."
- ➤ Fear of their employees: "I am not able to influence them to accept my change of behaviour and approach."
- ➤ Fear of risk: "My current results are OK, why jeopardise them?"
- ➤ Fear of being upstaged by you: "I am seen as having a good competency rating and if this manager intro-

duces coaching it may endanger that."

➤ Fear of appearing weak: "As a manager I have to be strong. Listening to others and allowing people to make their own decisions is a sign of weakness in me. As the boss I have to be seen as the strong decision maker."

It is frightening, isn't it? And I am sure there are many other fears and insecurities. In order for your peers to accept coaching you will have to minimise these fears. Keep them informed about what you are doing and why. Coaching will empower them to allow people to improve their capabilities and their performance. The result is an organisation that becomes profitable with less stress. Absenteeism and attrition will decrease. Keep statistics.

If senior management supports you, your position will be easier. You may, however, have to watch out for the odd manager who will want you to fail because they want the status quo to remain. Get as many fellow managers on your side as possible. The best way though is to link your coaching approach to the results that you gain.

I have been accused in the past by some individuals, as being a weak manager because I have taken what I call a people-centred approach. Yes, as a manager, my development areas were monitoring and budgeting, but I could never describe myself as weak just because I listened to and attempted to understand what was going on with the people on my team. I could be tough when it was appropriate or deserved and I have had the displeasure of disciplining people when necessary and of terminating contracts. I had no qualms about doing this, but only did it after reasons for under-performance were understood and after supportive measures to help people improve were not acted upon by the individual. Coaching is not a weakness; it is a strength.

Individuals on the Team – The Coachees

The biggest block for people when accepting coaching is trust, but there are other blocks. Some perceive coaching as therapy or counselling. Getting coaching appears to some that one is in need of correction or a fear that coaching will bring things to the surface that may alienate or embarrass them. This is simply not true.

The coachees have to fully understand what coaching is and most importantly what it is not. This is the first responsibility of any manager who starts to coach and uses the word "coach." Explain to them specifically what coaching is, the benefits, and what is involved. Engage their hearts and minds to realise coaching is a catalyst for action and success. There will always be a few sceptics but once you demonstrate the skills and maintain the contract you put in place, trust will grow and even the most difficult person will eventually see the benefits.

Regardless of where the blocks are, whether it is at senior level, peer management, or coachee level, use your coaching skills to define coaching, how and when it happens, and what results can be gained from taking a coaching approach. Demonstrate your skills, maintain the agreed contract, and show that the results gained are linked to the coaching interventions. When people realise that coaching is a strength and not a weakness or a threat they will be sold on it.

Not only do some see coaching as a sign of weakness, some see habits as weaknesses, too. The next chapter will demonstrate that habits can actually be strengths.

CHAPTER 12

The 7 Habits of Effective Coaching Managers

Steven Covey wrote a remarkable book called *The 7 Habits of Highly Effective People*, and if you haven't read it, I recommend it. It emphasises what individuals must do, and how they must behave in order to be successful. Similarly, I have looked at the habits of good, effective, coaching managers and I have developed a list of the 7 Habits of Effective Coaching Managers:

1. **Constantly Build Rapport Through Contracting and Re-contracting**

   The effective coaching manager is skilled in identifying different behaviour styles and can flex their own style to build rapport with other people. This ability to flex is consistent even through periods of stress and tension. In the initial stages of working with someone, the effective coaching manager will take time to contract so both sides can enter into an agreement where expectations are understood. The effective coaching manager can also identify when a contract needs reviewing either because one party has broken it or because the current contract is not working well.

2. **Ensures Own Objectives and Those of Subordinates are Clear and Understood**

A manager has to have focus and clarity about what he is striving to achieve and determine the best way to achieve goals. An effective coaching manager will take time to be sure all subordinates have clarity and focus regarding their business and personal objectives. A coaching manager will challenge and support both the reality of the objectives as well as the processes put in place to reach goals.

3. **Routinely Review and Update Personal Plans and Objectives as Well as Those of Subordinates**
An effective coaching manager will not only put clear plans in place and support the development of their subordinate's plans, they will also schedule regular reviews and adjust their own plans.

4. **Ensure Balance Between Management and Leadership**
Too often managers do not achieve balance between management and leadership. Broadly speaking some managers are happier stuck in front of their plans and their spreadsheets than spending time with their team and the individuals in the team. Some are exactly the opposite. An effective coaching manager will ensure that all management tasks are completed routinely and efficiently while preserving the right amount of time for listening to, motivating, coaching, and leading people.

5. **Prioritise Time Spent on Tasks, Team, and Individuals**
An effective coaching manager will be able to strike a balance in time spent on tasks, team meetings, and meetings with individuals. Too many managers think by organising team meetings on a regular basis that this will be all the

interaction that members of the team need. Individual meetings have to take place and an effective coaching manager will find a balance.

6. **Make Sure Time is Spent With Each Individual and the Correct Coaching Approach is Used**

   Individual meetings with each team member are essential if the coaching manager is going to help with and support the development of that individual. The correct approach that should be used with each member depends on the individual's stage on the Skill/Will Matrix. A temptation that many managers face is to treat all members the same within the team, and this approach tends to be advice giving or in some cases do as I say. This happens when their skills and motivation are not properly assessed; they may be given too little or too much responsibility.

7. **Lead the Way in Giving Constructive Feedback and Getting Personal Feedback from Superiors, Peers, and Subordinates**

   This is a huge development area for everybody. Most of us - although I have met some managers who are not - are very good at giving praise but many of us do not want to give constructive or critical feedback. An effective coaching manager is skilled at both, giving and receiving feedback. They also ask for feedback regularly. Not just from their superiors, but also from their peers and subordinates. Many times managers think because they are the boss they do not need to ask for feedback from subordinates. This is nonsense!

In Summary:

➤ Build rapport and contract
➤ Clarify and agree on objectives

- Regularly review progress
- Ensure balance between leadership and management
- Prioritise between task, team and individual
- Spend time with individuals and adopt appropriate approach
- Give and receive feedback

CHAPTER 13

A Question of Motivation

A former manager from my early days as a sales manager noticed that I had the ability to enthuse and energise my sales team. He asked me how I did it. I had not really thought about it and it was not until I started to analyse what I was doing that it occurred me what I was doing right. There were a number of things I was doing wrong, too, but we will look at that later.

I asked my team for feedback about what I was doing right when motivating them to work harder and more effectively. This is what they said:

➢ I took time away from the tasks of the everyday job to sit down with people.
➢ I listened to, and tried to understand what their hopes and fears were.
➢ I asked for their opinions on work related matters.
➢ I asked what their motivators and de-motivators were.
➢ I managed to link the tasks of the workplace to the benefits to be gained by the individuals.
➢ I lead by example in attitude and behaviour.
➢ I was trusted and trustworthy due to my honesty and accountability.

I also asked what they thought I was not doing right in terms of motivating them. They said:

➤ I wasn't very good at outlining boundaries. People sometimes did not know where they stood.
➤ I trusted people too much.
➤ I tended to rebel against senior management instead of "managing" them effectively.
➤ I tended to give advice and tell people what to do instead of guiding them to formulate their own conclusions. I had a "blanket" approach regarding the way I dealt with people. In other words I wasn't really coaching.
➤ I wasn't very effective when interacting with administration.

What does this have to do with motivation? I started to examine this feedback and I could see that if I continued some behaviours and adapted or changed others I would be able to motivate all individuals in the team, and sustain that momentum. The incentive for me was a motivated, responsible, and accountable team who would be productive. This would allow more time for me to concentrate on strategy and facilitating forward movement of the business, instead of conflict resolution and stress management. As a result of improved performance, I could enjoy my time at work more and make more money.

To add validity to my coaching approach, I linked this feedback to models of motivation developed by experts in the field. It would be impossible to review all of the models that have evolved on the subject of motivation in this small book, and some of them only confuse rather than enlighten. But I have found two models very useful in helping me understand what it takes to motivate an individual or a whole team. They are *Maslow's Hierarchy of Needs* and *The Motivational Triangle*.

Maslow's Hierarchy of Needs. Abraham Maslow (1908–70, an American psychologist and a central figure in the human potential movement) developed a model for motivation which became known as Maslow's Hierarchy of Needs. This is a well-known model, which can be found in books authored by Maslow, books written by his supporters, as well as in textbooks about coaching and motivation.

This hierarchy is usually depicted as a pyramid with five levels, ranging from the most basic needs – physiological needs – at the bottom, to the most complex and sophisticated needs – self actualisation at the top with the other three levels filling in the middle. According to his theory, when their most basic needs are met humans will search for self-esteem and self-actualisation. From bottom to top, the levels are these:

➢   Physiological – food, water, sleep, warmth
➢   Safety/Security – freedom from fear and violence, shelter, order
➢   Belonging – friendship, being in a family, group or team, social acceptance
➢   Self-Esteem – self-respect, status, being valued by others
➢   Self-Actualisation – need for challenge, variety and growth and need to reach one's full potential.

The goal is to coach people at whatever level of Maslow's hierarchy they are in at the present time and help them to "move to the next level" when they are ready. Most people in a work situation will be well above the physiological and safety/security stage with some aspiring towards self-actualisation.

I have seen people fluctuate between the Belonging level and the Self-Actualisation level when they are new employees in the company.

Although they might have been operating at the Self-Actualisation level with their previous employers, they may for a time be several steps down on the hierarchy, for example, they may be in the third level: Belonging. Usually this is due to an initial lack of acceptance or welcome from the new team.

To motivate these people you would not begin by giving them challenging tasks, because you would potentially de-motivate them. What they need is a chance to become accepted in their new environment. They need to be introduced to work colleagues and superiors, to learn their new jobs and make friends at work. Once they are established with their peers and their work expectations they can move to the next level: Self Esteem. When this level is achieved and the new employee is assimilated in their new place with the help of a nurturing, supportive, coach they may eventually be ready to move towards Self-Actualisation. This is the level all organisations should be aiming to get their employees into and then maintain them there.

I have seen previous employers lose a number of top quality people, people who were in the Self-Actualisation level. These people appeared to have slipped down the hierarchy towards the Self-Esteem level and in some cases to the Belonging level. This happens when management is not using their employees' full potential by including them in decision -making and other situations that would give them more responsibility. The management of the company, for example, may have been experiencing problems from a transition after a merger. The manager may have assumed that because these people were "top class" they would "continue to perform with little guidance." If this is the case then the management team has missed a vital step in motivating employees by making assumptions about people's level of motivation. Again communication skills, such as, feedback, listening, and coping with stress might have helped in this case. The second model I am using is:

The Motivational Triangle. This model was introduced to me by Brian Whittle, the former Great Britain Olympic 4 × 400 meters gold medallist, who I had the pleasure of sharing a stage with in 2002. It is a simplistic model, but, for me, it sums up motivation perfectly. I now use this model routinely in my coaching sessions. There are three points to this triangle:

1. **Freedom to Choose**

    In any role there will be guidelines and boundaries. Once people know exactly what they are, then it is the role of the manager to enable and support the employee to make decisions on their own within these boundaries. Giving people a choice will enable them to feel ownership and hence motivation. Continually telling people what to do and not giving a choice will result in de-motivation.

2. **Understanding and Being Understood**

    How many times have you had an employee, despite your telling them what to do, go away, and do something different? In this case, you may be left to pick up the pieces. You are de-motivated and so are they. It is vital that you take time as a manager to fully understand your people and their circumstances. If something goes wrong, do not blame. Seek to find out exactly what went wrong and what can be done to prevent reoccurrence. I have come across numerous examples, where the root cause of an issue lies, not with what the employee has or hasn't done, but with improper communication from the manager. It is important for the employer and employees to understand expectations.

3. **Being Valued**

    Praise is the most powerful form of feedback and as managers we do not use it enough. We seem to have an attitude that says, "Why should I praise someone for doing a job that is expected of them?" What does it cost to say two small words – "Thank you?"

I addressed this at a seminar I lead recently, and a manager said, "What happens if you are observing a salesperson and nothing goes right at all. How can you start to praise?" At first, my answer was a challenge to the manager because how could he be sure that absolutely nothing went right? Then I asked him, "Did the salesperson not even make an effort to get the sale?" The manager's reply was, "Of course he did." "So," I asked, "Why not praise him for making an effort, and then help him explore what did not go as well as it should have and what the potential reasons were for this?"

We all need to feel valued in some way and it does not take very much for the manager to say "thank you" or "well done."

When things go wrong it is tempting to rid yourself of possible ridicule. It is tempting to blame someone else. Next we will see why that is one of the worst ways to uncover a solution.

CHAPTER 14

7 Points About Blame

One of the worst behaviours a manager can display is blame. How often have you had a manager blame you when something went wrong? How did that feel? How often have you been in meetings where perhaps a team is not doing well with its objectives and the manager puts the blame firmly at the feet of the team members?

The manager who blames is not a coaching manager and until the manager takes responsibility for what is happening in any situation instead of blaming, he or she will not show great leadership.

What should a coaching manager do in order to avoid blaming team members, or anyone else for that matter? Here are some suggestions:

1.   **Be Aware**
     Too often we fail to notice that we are placing the blame. It is a natural defence mechanism. Paying attention to how we respond when questioned about our actions or performance is the first step in taking responsibility.

2.   **Be Responsible in Your Response**
     Just as blaming is a defensive move, so is reacting. Rather than react you should stop and think before you respond. We

normally want to react immediately with a burst of anger, but instead train your-self to stop and consider the choices. We have a choice of reacting impulsively or responding cautiously to the situation. What will your choice be?

3. **Honesty is the Best Policy**
    Let's face it; some people simply like to place blame in order to be relieved of responsibility. That shows a huge lack of self-honesty and a distinct lack of accountability. By saying, "It's my responsibility" or "It was my fault it didn't happen" your credibility as a manager and as a person is secured with those you manage and with your superiors.

4. **Avoid Alienation**
    What happens to relationships when you place blame? You are unlikely to earn forgiveness. You are more likely to alienate yourself from your colleagues, superiors, customers, and others when you point fingers. Not only will you ruin relationships, but you will also lose the trust of your co-workers.

5. **Lead by Example**
    When others see you accepting responsibility for your actions – and when they see the extraordinary results you are getting – you make the statement that placing blame is not acceptable behaviour. By doing this, you help promote an atmosphere of harmony and integrity.

6. **Have a Positive Attitude**
    Being a progressive coaching manager means being a highly effective leader, and accepting nothing less than excellence from yourself and others. If you are grateful for all the things that happen in your life – good and bad – you simply cannot hold angry feelings toward others, or place blame where it does not belong. It takes practice to reach that level, but

coaching managers understand that the investment is well worth it.

7. **Challenge Those Who Blame**
    If you have employees who, when challenged or asked about their actions, start to blame others or events for either the action or inaction, challenge them. Get them to stop and think and then coach them to get to the root of the problem. Help them to accept the real reasons and who is responsible. By doing this you will raise their awareness.

In Summary:

- ➢   Be Aware
- ➢   Be Responsible
- ➢   Be Honest
- ➢   Avoid Alienation
- ➢   Lead By Example
- ➢   Be Positive
- ➢   Challenge those who blame

Sometimes blame occurs as a direct reaction to stress. Everyone is at risk and it can cause us to do things we would not normally do. The next chapter addresses stress and what we can do to cope with it in our workers and us.

CHAPTER 15

The Challenge of Stress

In every organisation employees are at risk from stress. Change of role, working conditions, downsizing, right-sizing, threat of redundancy, bad management, collapse of relationships, and mergers are just a few of the factors that can cause stress levels to rise in individuals. Almost any kind of change – good or bad – can lead to varying levels of stress in individuals. The role of the coaching manager concerning stress is two fold:

1. To recognise when their employees are under stress and,
2. To support them through these periods. It is imperative for a coaching manager to be sure that they do not cause the stress. There are some instances where stress cannot be avoided but in many cases it is actually the behaviour of the manager that is the root cause in the first place. At the same time, management is a stressful role and managers have to be on the lookout for signs of stress within themselves and others.

Stress becomes apparent through both physical and psychological symptoms. It can manifest itself as high blood pressure, ulcers, weight gain or loss, sleep deprivation, irritability, depression, migraines, asthma, drug and alcohol dependence, mental exhaustion, the list goes on. I sadly have seen all of these symptoms during my time in management. I have also suffered at the hand of stress myself, so I know how it feels firsthand.

Stress is the largest cause of work absenteeism and causes billions of dollars of lost business revenue very year. The effects of stress on British Industry are huge. Low performance, low self-esteem and reduced productivity have contributed to a loss of revenue in Britain. (£10.2bn in lost productivity in 1998 alone as reported by the CBI). A report by MORI November 1999 showed 60% of the working population is affected by stress at work.

Job stress has been estimated to cost American industry $150 billion per year in absenteeism, diminished productivity, compensation claims, health insurance and direct medical expenses. To get some perspective, these costs are more than 15 times that of all strikes combined.

What can the coaching manager do to lessen the incidence and impact of stress within the workforce? The coaching manager should remember some important points about stress:

➢ Stress can kill.
➢ Suffering from stress should not be considered a weakness.
➢ Stress is infectious. It is stressful to live and work with people who are suffering from stress.
➢ Stress is produced by high demands and lack of support.
➢ There are numerous techniques that can minimise stress.

The following tips should help managers not only relieve stress for employees but in many cases prevent it or its debilitating effects.

➢   Watch for signs of stress in employees. Notice their behaviour, mannerisms, changes in appearance, and absenteeism record.

➢   If you suspect any of your employees are suffering the effects of stress take time to talk with them.

➢   Get feedback from them about what they think needs to change in order for them to "get back to normal."

➢   Use coaching and counselling techniques to assess and help them through tough times, but set boundaries. If the situation starts to border on "therapy" then do not hesitate to refer them to someone fully qualified. Do not, under any circumstances, attempt to become a "part time or amateur therapist."

➢   Let them know you are empathetic to their situation and if they need time-off from work, they should be allowed to have it.

As far as prevention of stress a manager should consider these questions:

➢   What is the exact cause of the stress? Is it organisational, for example, a threat of merger, role change, redundancy, working conditions, or management style? Or is it strictly personal?

➢   If it is personal then consider referring them to a professional counsellor depending on the nature of the issue. I have supported people through challenges with their marriages that were causing a negative impact on their working lives. I only achieved this through a high degree of trust. If you do not have this trust with the employee then you will struggle to support people through home life challenges. Again keep the boundaries.

If it is organisationally based, what can you do about it?

- Some aspects of organisational change will not go away and the manager has to be able to support employees through the change. This can be done by keeping communication as open and frequent as possible, ensuring that people are kept up to date with all developments.

- If the stress is due to working conditions or management style then the manager can certainly try to do something. Listen to what the employee thinks is causing the stress and attempt to be as empathetic as possible. Do not agree with the complaints, but certainly empathise. There will be certain things you cannot change and if you agree with the employee's complaint then you will not move that person forward because they will feel that you are supporting them regarding that complaint.

- Help them to look at their options. Help them decide how can they deal with the situation and then coach them to action. If the stress is caused by you as a manager, then seek to understand exactly what the behaviours are that are causing the stress. Change them if it is appropriate. Most competent managers will be aware of the impact they are having on employees and will change behaviours where appropriate.

CHAPTER 16

The Coaching Manager – Case Studies

Case Study No.1 – Malcolm

Malcolm is in his late twenties and has just moved into a management role. He has been trying to get into management for a few years. He was becoming bored in his old sales executive role. He has inherited the team that he used to be part of and he thinks this will be good for the team. There had been disquiet among the team with little respect for the previous manager. Malcolm gets along well with all his team colleagues and he did not think they would have any problems accepting him as their new boss. After all, he knew what they disliked about the last manager.

Malcolm started his new role with a team meeting and proceeded to run the meetings just like normal. Sales statistics, customer activities, and promotional campaigns were all on the agenda. There was also a review of the new sales aids. It was as if nothing had changed from the old manager to the new.

At one meeting a team member asked how he was going to change things based on the fact that Malcolm himself had been uncomfortable with the way the team had been run by the previous manager. Malcolm replied that since he was new to the job he wasn't going to change things overnight and that there was a job that needed to be done in the area of sales. He also said the meeting had to finish on time because he had a plane to catch to get to the head office.

Malcolm's last duty in the meeting was to arrange field visits with each sales representative and dates were duly entered into the diary. Malcolm did explain that he might not be able to keep every field visit date because of meetings and he also said that some field visits would only be a couple of hours in length because he had to look at sales figures and business plans. A comment made at the end of the meeting he did not hear was, "No change from the last manager!"

Over the first few weeks, Malcolm kept up regular communication with the team via the telephone, but the field visits that he had promised never materialised. He kept himself busy, either attending meetings or at home working on business plans. This caused frustration with some members of the team, particularly the younger ones. The older sales executives were quite happy because it left them in peace. When Malcolm finally did visit his representatives he concentrated on visiting only a portion of the team. This caused confusion; they wondered why some were getting visits and others were not. It appeared he was visiting the younger ones who he had some influence over and that he was avoiding the more experienced sales executives. This resulted in some team discontent. Some thought he was favouring the older sales executives and as a result, was being manipulated by them. What should Malcolm have done to make his transition into management easier for himself and the team?

1. **Sought a coach and mentor**

   In the absence of support he should have been pro-active in finding senior manager support to help him get through the early days of his new position. Competent senior managers could have made sure everyone was involved and accounted for. Sadly, many senior managers think that putting a new manager on a two, three, or four-day course with no follow up will turn new managers into superstars overnight. This does not happen and new managers should be given either internal support through a mentor manager or given some form of external coaching resource.

2.   **Be vulnerable**

This is a big step. Malcolm should have met with his team both on a one to one basis and as a team to discuss how his employees were feeling about him as the new manager. He could ask questions of them, such as, what are your expectations, hopes, and fears? He could share his expectations, hopes, and fears in a mutual exchange. Many managers go straight into management positions and continue to operate the way the previous manager did because they think that is what is expected. The new manager must make a new contract with the team.

3.   **Contract**

What are his expectations of the way they are going to work together? Malcolm should be managing each and every one of his team's expectations. He should be creating boundaries within which each member can work flexibly. Few managers discuss and agree to a working contract with their teams. Once a manager and his subordinates know where they stand with each other and know what each other's expectations are, then a profitable working relationship can commence.

4.   **Face the Fear**

Malcolm was enjoying his new-found fame, and the lure of important activities that took him away from his team, such as head office meetings and business planning. These activities are important but they are intended to enhance a manager's relationship with the team not take from it. Although it is exciting to move into new areas of work, a manager must maintain a balance between administrative duties, and supporting and leading the team. Failure to achieve this balance will result in frustration, and low production in all areas.

When Malcolm finally got back to leading the team, he moved towards the newer, less experienced salespeople and away from the older, more vocal and opinionated ones. He liked the fact that the newer people looked to him for advice. He disliked the rookie status he felt he had with the older more experienced people. He felt they were continually complaining about the car policy, or evening meeting allowances, for example. If he had scheduled the discussion meetings according to the format above, and contracted with his employees he could have avoided all this. Malcolm would have been able to interact with each sales executive without fear and trepidation.

Malcolm did achieve the balance between working with the Head Office/Senior Management, customers, and leading and developing the team which resulted in his profile being raised within the company overall. He ended up being respected by all members of his team, because they knew his expectations, he remained consistent in his approach. He became a great coach.

Case Study No. 2 – James

James is in his late thirties and has been a manager for ten years. He had been an average performer in his last role, even though some of his business skills are excellent. James is very efficient: he builds and maintains his business and manages his time effectively. He is a man who sets high standards for himself as well as others. When members of his team do not meet these standards, however, he becomes frustrated and tends to either shout a lot, or worse, goes to senior management and complains about the "idiots" he has inherited. This behaviour is supported by some of the senior managers although others in top management positions are questioning James' ability to support and develop his employees.

James' behaviour is having a detrimental effect on team morale. He is simply not trusted. He appears to say one thing to one person and a different thing to another. He also tries to find out what people "are up to, or not up to," by skillfully asking questions and catching them "unaware." He does not confront individuals about his concerns but rather takes a "back door" approach to find out exactly what his employees "are up to."

Despite his assumed time management skills, he does not take time to meet with, and spend quality time with his people. He tells people what to do instead of using a coaching approach with them. He apparently feels, "It's easier to tell them what to do, rather than wait for them to come up with an answer on their own."

Needless to say, James is losing his team fast. They resent him because it is up to them as individuals to get work done and not a result of his management and leadership (or lack of it). They are succeeding in spite of him, but they are not a cohesive group working together. If they functioned as a team, they would be more productive with reduced stress.

Some senior managers are not happy with James' performance because his previous good capability rating is now being questioned as a result of his behaviour and the obvious disgruntlement within the team.

How can James save himself and become a coaching manager?

James has some bridge building to do with his reputation at an all time low with his team and with senior managers starting to question his ability. James needs constructive feedback. He will not get it from his team right now. Even if he does he is not likely to listen. There is even less chance that he would put the feedback to good use right now anyway because of his attitude.

Senior managers need to give James this feedback. They must make him aware of the impact and the implications of his behaviour on the business as well as the individuals. If there are competency frameworks in place, then James' competencies need to be reassessed. Only then will he realise that he has to change his behaviour.

When James understands this, he has to be open with his team and tell them that he realises his behaviour has affected the team and the business. It will be necessary for him to contract individually with each team member outlining how they are going to work together and how this will be different from the past. Within this contract James needs to evoke accurate constructive feedback when he asks for it. He must respond to it in a way that will help him and the team to improve and grow.

James must promise himself and his team that he will live up to these agreements. By doing this, in time he will regain the trust of his team. This will demand a commitment on his part because it could take only one slip and any trust that has built up could vanish — forever.

James will also have to contract with some of the senior managers and perhaps break some of the ties he has had with others. He will have to pay particular attention to those managers who have tolerated his complaining about the team. He should be coached by senior management to change his ways, and not have his bad behaviour supported.

He also needs to ensure that he gets the right balance between spending time on planning and reviewing plans with spending time listening to and developing his team members. His strengths are evident in planning, but he has to work on his people skills: rapport building, contracting and coaching. James should build a personal development plan that reflects his strategies in these areas.

James must let himself be vulnerable. He must face reality and change and develop accordingly. This may take time, but if he gets support from senior management, re-contracts with his team and maintains that contract, things will begin to happen for James.

If he does not get constructive feedback from his peers and superiors will James will probably never change.

Case Study No. 3 – Jenny

Jenny has been a manager for four years. She is well liked by most of her team and by her peers. Her teams have tended to be successful because she has excellent recruitment skills. Her superiors are concerned, however, that Jenny takes on too much, particularly where the team is concerned. She gets caught up in the everyday tasks that the team has to perform and does a lot of work herself, when instead she should be delegating more. Senior management would like her to use her talents on more strategic issues rather than everyday tasks. When she does delegate she tends assign tasks to team members without offering them much support.

She is seen, though, as someone who spends time with the individuals on the team and appears to be a good listener. Jenny does gossip, however. Some well-intentioned coaching sessions with her team members rapidly turn into unproductive moaning or gossiping sessions. She has also been accused of showing favouritism, since she meets more regularly with, and socialises with selected individuals of her team. This is starting to create factions within the team.

Jenny has some superb talents, so how can she develop into an effective and even more productive coaching manager?

She has recruited a highly capable and apparently motivated productive team. But she has specific behaviour she must adjust in order to continue developing and growing her team towards being even more successful.

She is obviously good at building rapport but she takes this stage too far. She is too "friendly" and not assertive enough. She needs to distinguish rapport from friendliness. She must ensure that a productive and mutually agreed upon contract is established between her and each of her team members. She needs to set boundaries in which they can operate. For example, a one to one coaching session should be used to focus on the individual's objectives and strategies for development not used as a gossiping session. Jenny will have to tighten up her contracting and set an example with her behaviours.

Developing her knowledge of the Skill/Will or Capability/Motivation Matrix, and using the appropriate intervention when dealing with each of her team members will benefit her. It is necessary for her to delegate appropriately and learn when to coach, guide, and direct. Right now it seems she does everything herself, unless it is a task that she does not like or is not capable of doing. Jenny must delegate responsibility. Failure to use the correct approach with these individuals could result in de-motivation and frustration for her and team members.

She may have to look at either her time management or her beliefs about herself and /or members of her team. She may want to ask herself these questions. When a team member asks for her support on a task that they are actually capable of doing themselves, can she say no, and support them to do it rather than doing it for them? What are the things that keep Jenny internally focused within the team, rather than directing her focus towards customers and the company? Self-belief? Lack of knowledge or capability? Her senior manager should be supporting her to decipher the exact reasons for this and then support her to develop her capabilities and confidence in this area.

Jenny should obliterate her reputation of showing favouritism. She should treat each of her team members equally and, as we discussed above, she should choose the appropriate intervention in this area. The Capability/Motivation Grid is useful here as well. Involving herself in gossip needs to stop immediately. Her professional standing as a manager will collapse if this is not done.

Jenny will become a more productive coaching manager when she masters these objectives:

➤ Distinguishes between rapport and friendliness and practices it accordingly.
➤ Builds a sound and professional contract between herself and her team members.
➤ Improves time management and beliefs around the capability of her team. She should perhaps work with a coach or seek a mentor from her senior management group.
➤ Uses the capability/motivation grid more appropriately.
➤ Uses her good listening skills and ensures one to one coaching meetings have both a business and developmental purpose.
➤ Stop favouritism and gossiping.

Case Study No. 4 – Brian

Brian has been a manager for four years and has been fairly

successful. He does not contribute often at meetings and does not socialise with the other managers very much. He feels more comfortable being with his team than with his peers.

His team likes him because he is very supportive, but there is frustration. His approach is the same with everyone on the team and he seems incapable of adapting to meet the individual needs and styles of each team member. Brian is not an assertive manager. He prefers to take a "laid back," facilitative approach. This has gotten him in trouble in the past. He has had to put some of his team on the company disciplinary process after some irregularities occurred in the way they were doing business. Brian's team has a reputation for doing their "own thing" instead of following company policies. A recent survey of Brian's team found that 75% of the members did not follow the rules because they did not know what they were. Of the 25% who did know the rules only half of them adhered to them because Brian is seen as an "easy touch" when it comes to discipline so they did not worry about it.

Brian's customers think he is fantastic because he provides excellent customer service.

Senior management is beginning to have concerns about his overall capability given the disciplinary record of some of the members in his team.

What can Brian do to become a more effective manager?

Brian has to go back and ensure that the operational guidelines laid down by the organisation are understood and adhered to. Brian has never liked rules, but he needs to follow them to raise his profile within his team. He likes to be seen as a rebel by his team, but he has kept this quiet from his superiors and peers.

Brian needs to change this aspect of his behaviour; he and his team have suffered the consequences of failing to respect authority. In order to do this, Brian needs to talk to his team on a one to one basis and re-contract their roles to establish a working relationship that is productive and mindful of company policy. Brian needs to make his team members understand that he will follow the company's policies. He needs to make them aware of potential consequences of the team not operating according to the organisation's guidelines.

Brian's support for his team is great, however he needs to be flexible in his behaviours so that he can address them as the individuals they are rather than treating them all the same like he does now. He needs to assess each one's position on the Capability/Motivation Grid and decide which type of coaching approach is best for that individual based on the discussions he has with them. By building in coaching time he will be in a position to continue to support his team but in a much more assertive way than supporting them from a distance where he doesn't always know what is happening with each of them.

Brian has a good facilitative style and he could benefit from enhancing his skills in this area by perhaps enrolling in a coaching course. Behavioural analysis study could also benefit him in this aspect.

Brian also needs to raise his profile within his peer management group and with his superiors. He would learn from constructive feedback from this group what they perceive his qualities and development areas to be. He should also re-contract with his superiors to outline their expectations of him and decipher the best way for them to work together.

Another area he should develop is his assertiveness within the group. He has plenty of good creative ideas but does not feel confident enough to present them to the group. Working with a coach or mentor (perhaps a superior) would help Brian to overcome these fears.

Case Study No. 5 – Julie

Julie had been promoted from trainer to manager and is very ambitious. She had a mixed reputation as a trainer, in that she appeared to be knowledgeable about her subjects although there were doubts about her actual training and people skills. When she ever had issues with the people she was training, instead of managing and resolving the issues herself, she would immediately turn to senior management in order for them to personally sort out the situation on her behalf. This caused mistrust on her behalf from her employees.

There was a fear within her new team that she would abuse her new-found power that came with her promotion. Unfortunately, the team's fears materialised. Julie immediately held a team meeting and spelled out, in no uncertain terms, how she wanted the team to operate. She assured them she was going to be a tough, but fair manager and she was going to run a "tight ship" making sure the rules were adhered to and budgets strictly scrutinised. There would be no repetition of the lax way the previous manager had managed the team. Results were everything and if any member of the team "slacked" in the pursuit of results and excellence, disciplinary action was certain.

This left the team in a bit of a "cold sweat." The last manager had been a bit lax in certain areas but he was fair and just. He had spent time with each individual, coaching and guiding them to success. The team had been successful in most areas. They just needed to improve on a few things. Their reaction, although they agreed things could be improved and they had been prepared to work on them for the old manager, was that they were not going to "jump to attention" immediately for what they perceived was an immature beginner.

The first team meeting was a disaster for Julie. She controlled the gathering, but whenever she ask for feedback from the team to fulfil a request from the Head Office she got little response and as a result she concocted the feedback to save her face. Similarly when she held individual meetings, she ended up doing all the "telling" because for the few questions she asked she received little response. Nobody did any wrong but creativity, innovation, and feedback all but disappeared.

Julie grew frustrated about the lack of response from her team. She revisited some old behaviour and went straight to senior management to complain that she had inherited a "bunch of duffers" and that she could not believe how the previous manager had been able to get away with recruiting them. She demanded that senior management do something.

The Result?

Julie got a shock! The new senior manager would take no action to change her team members. It was Julie's responsibility to manage and motivate the team management had given her. They felt she had inherited a good team, albeit a bit slack in some areas. But overall they performed well, and were successful.

The senior manager had been watching the change and decided to confront Julie at this point about the way she handled her team. The manager asked these questions: How had she contracted her role with the team and with each individual in the team? Had she managed their expectations? Did she for that matter know what their expectations were? How were they feeling about losing their old boss? How did they feel about the new manager? What were their hopes and fears? How were they all going to work together? What did the team each individual want to achieve this year? What were they good at? What did they need to improve?

Julie suddenly realised she had asked no questions – she had dictated. She presumed that her way was best and it was simpler and easier to tell them what to do than to sit down and take time with each individual. After all they were only employees and she had more important managerial tasks to perform.

The senior manager started to question her beliefs about people and after some skillful questioning challenged those beliefs. "If these beliefs are real then you have no place as a manager and leader of people," he told her. Julie thought carefully and admitted that she had taken the dictatorial approach, not because of the lack of time, but because she had feared having to manage conflict, both with her team and with her superior. When he said, "jump" Julie, said "how high" because she had feared him. If the team were given the "freedom to choose" and their way was different from the senior manager, she felt that it would make her look bad. She feared that the manager would think that she could not control the team and that the team controlled her. She feared she might lose the position and she had worked so hard to get promoted.

The new senior manager consoled her, helped her regain her composure and then coached her, helping her find ways to work with her team. She had to admit to the team that her approach had been wrong and that she had seen the error of her ways. She had to make herself vulnerable and confide in them about the reasons she had acted the way she did. She re-contracted with each individual to find out what their needs, aspirations, and motivations were, as well as discussing her own. They agreed how they were going to work together and how they were going to give feedback to each other.

Julie duly did all this, and the team were sceptical at first, because they did not trust her. She was true to her word and she kept the contracts that had been put in place. She also contracted with the senior manager who acted as her coach and mentor and this relationship worked well. Julie developed rapidly into a fine coaching manager whose team was ultimately very successful.

Case Study No. 6 – Gerald

Gerald has been a manager for ten years now after a very successful period as a representative within the same company. His team has been relatively successful and his turnover of representatives has been fairly low. Gerald has been described as "solid" and "dependable" without being outstanding. His most recent boss was very laid back and basically let Gerald "get on with it". However, times are changing. His company has been merged with a larger rival and Gerald has found himself with a new senior manager, Colin, and a dramatically different culture than the one he knows and is comfortable with. He also has some new colleagues to work with and there is a chance that he may lose some of his old team and have to take on new representatives from the other company. Gerald is confused and very nervous although he has been confirmed as not being one of those who will be made redundant.

Gerald's first meeting with Colin left him even more nervous. This new lad was a completely different "kettle of fish" from his last boss. He was young and dynamic: he talked in terms of a new beginning, new processes with new rewards. Gerald found him quite refreshing and he reminded him of how he himself used to be in his early management days before apathy had set in. Gerald remembered his own early vision of self-directed teams, peer reviews where the reps had a major say in each other's appraisals, and generally a more empowered environment. However he had lost that drive a long time ago due to senior management failing to heed his pleas and proposals and for the last four or five years he had basically "coasted". Part of him was excited that perhaps his own visions of years ago could potentially come to fruition but the other part of him said that this new guy, Colin, was all talk and no substance. Perhaps it was just best to keep quiet and hope that things remained the same as they always had been.

What could Colin have done to get Gerald "on board" right from their first meeting? The fact that Gerald left the meeting with his fears still intact meant that Colin had missed an opportunity to get Gerald's "buy in" to the new vision right from the "word go". Colin had obviously been dynamic and had impressed Gerald with the presentation of his vision but he had not exactly been a listener. He should have engaged Gerald in a two-way conversation finding out more about him and how Gerald was feeling about the merger and future. If Colin had done his research perhaps he may have found out a bit more about Gerald's past and that in this man, there was actually a potential ally in helping him make his vision a reality. Instead the only information Colin gleaned was that Gerald's recent performance was slightly above average and that he was "solid" and "dependable". Looking further into the past might have saved Colin valuable time in getting Gerald fully "on board". Even if he was unable to access this information about Gerald's past, simply by engaging Gerald in a two-way conversation and through exploring how Gerald was feeling about what was happening, then Colin could have tapped into Gerald's suppressed personal visions for the business, which appear not to be too far away from Colin's own. This first meeting was a fantastic chance to motivate a capable individual and to ensure that he had support to move the company vision forward. Colin missed a golden opportunity simply by not gathering enough information, listening and asking exploratory questions.

What should Gerald have done to make the meeting more productive for himself? Gerald should have been more open. Obviously, had Colin been a better coach he would have paved the way for that openness to occur, but in this absence Gerald should have been more proactive. His job had been confirmed and a lot of what Colin was saying appealed to him. Instead of just listening he should have contributed more by voicing his opinions both in terms of supporting those points he agreed with and either challenged or explored further points that he disagreed with or was not 100% clear about.

This is a classic situation where new managers think that simply by being dynamic and presenting a wonderful picture of what the new environment is going to look like, they are going to get "buy in" from employees. It takes more than a dynamic and polished presentation to get people to commit to something new, particularly when what they hear and see is potentially very different from what they have been used to. People must be treated, as individuals and a manager must take each individual in their team through what the changes are and what these changes mean to them as individuals. People must understand exactly what is going on and they must be coached through the change process. Simply dictating is a recipe for disaster. Individuals also must stand up and "be counted". They have to communicate their concerns but only after they have fully explored and understood what the changes are and how they will be affected. More often than not, the rumour "mill" leads people to believe un-truths about exactly what is going on. This is neither helpful nor productive. If change is going to happen productively, managers must meet and listen to individuals in addition to presenting to them en-masse, and individuals within the teams must stand up and use these situations to get answers to their fears and concerns. Change is about pro-activity, communication and openness. Change is a partnership.

CHAPTER 17

The Coaching Manager – Holiday Reflections

I am a "people watcher" whether in a restaurant or waiting for a flight, I am always fascinated by people and the way they behave and react.

On a recent holiday trip to the Spanish Island of Fuerteventura, we ate in many cafes and restaurants. This provided me with many opportunities to observe the behaviours of both restaurant staff and customers. I saw some superb examples of coaching models in action that are explained in this book.

Contracting

There was one particular restaurateur who was excellent at contracting. He immediately greeted customers at the door as they wandered in, looking lost, with a cheery welcome. He introduced himself and asked them their names. He asked what sort of food they liked and where they would be most comfortable sitting.

On one particular evening, when the restaurant was busy, he also explained that perhaps service might not be a quick as usual due to the popularity of the restaurant that evening. Did anyone complain, or leave? Not that I saw.

What had this restaurateur done that could be applied to management and coaching?

1.   He put people at ease by smiling and including them. How often do we as managers put people at ease and make them feel included? How often have we left the new trainee to fend for herself on a month - long training course while we convinced ourselves that a new person's inclusion to the company is the responsibility of the Training Department? I know of a senior manager who will not be pro-active in introducing himself to subordinates. He feels since he is the boss, people should introduce themselves to him, not he to them. I am not sure if I agree with that one. What do you think?

2.   He managed their expectations when they knew exactly what kind of food he served and the level of service they could expect. How often as managers do we expect our employees to know how we operate as managers because they should "know what a boss does?"

Awareness

A waiter in another restaurant showed fantastic awareness of his customers. Not only did he check on his customers to ask how they liked the food and the service, he was constantly on the lookout for other signs of both dissatisfaction and satisfaction. If he noticed a facial expression that indicated the customer did not like the food he immediately tried to remedy the situation. On a couple of occasions I saw him replace the food. He paid attention to expressions that indicated the customer was delighted with their food too.

A personal example of his awareness was when I chose a port instead of ice cream for dessert. The port was consumed faster than the other desserts. The server noticed this and offered me another to enjoy while my family finished their desserts. A good example of awareness: filling a customer need and increasing sales!

As a manager or coach, how is your awareness of your own needs and the needs of your employees or people you coach? Are you constantly aware of their satisfactions and dissatisfactions? If you are not discerning facial expressions and body language are you asking them directly how things are going? Too many managers when asked how their employees are, and how well they are doing, do not really know. As a result, they make assumptions only to find out at their own cost later that something was wrong.

Responsibility

I saw both a good and bad example of responsibility on this holiday.

➤ The bad example was in a bar when the bottled beer ran out. The barman immediately blamed the suppliers when it turned out later that he had missed the order deadline. His credibility with me plummeted.

➤ The good example was with the man we rented our car from. He admitted that he had forgotten to include a booster seat for my five-year-old daughter and it was his fault. He promised he would rectify that immediately. He did not say, "We couldn't find the right one," or "Are you sure you asked for one?" His manner pleased us and his admission of responsibility helped calm our frustrations.

As a manager or coach do you take responsibility when things go wrong or do you tend to blame others when perhaps some of your actions or interventions may have been the cause? I have seen many examples over the years of managers blaming their representatives for a team's under-performance when perhaps they should have looked at their own behaviour and attitudes. I am always amazed at those sales managers who blame sales representatives for poor performance when they have recruited and chosen them themselves. On very few occasions have I ever seen a manager stand up and say, "I made a recruitment mistake there," or " I hold my hand up and admit I did not support the representative's development as much as I could have."

Praise

Praise is the most powerful form of feedback in terms of motivation. I saw a number of examples where no praise was given and one example of excellence in the form of praise. This example came from a restaurant manager who had high awareness as he monitored the movements of both customers and staff. He was obviously monitoring a couple of "trainee" waiters. On several occasions he intervened to adjust what the waiter was doing. He did it very supportively, always with a pat on the trainee's shoulder and a smile. Even when one young person dropped a knife near some customers he entered quickly offering support saying to the customers, "He is young, he learns, but he will be a great waiter!" Fantastic! How often do you praise your staff as a manager?

PART II

The Coaching Manager and Teams

CHAPTER 18

What is a Team?

Almost all managers will have a group of people to manage and coach and there will be many occasions where the manager will have the opportunity to "team coach".

This is an area of coaching skill, and in many cases, it is a far more difficult skill to grasp than just coaching an individual. I have seen many managers who have grasped the skill of one to one coaching fail in team situations and in many cases return to their old "dictatorial" ways simply because they did not know how to coach effectively in a team situation.

So where do you begin? There are numerous things about teams.

What specifically is a team? What makes a good team? What about team roles and mix of personalities? Team dynamics? Team Development? Problem Solving? Facilitation of the team?

In this chapter we will start with the basics and look at the few first steps the coaching manager can take in order to start to lead and coach their team.

It is important to firstly understand specifically what a team is. I have been amazed by the number of people I have encountered over the years that claim they know what a team is and when challenged to come up with a definition, struggle to do this. Many people think that just by working with a group of people that they are a team but if that group does not have a collective goal or objective then they are not a team, they are a work group. A team is a collection of people who are working towards a common goal or objective. There are two aspects to teams – the task or objective and the process or the way the individuals are going to work together to achieve the team's goals or objectives.

If the team is a new team, or if the manager is new to the team, then it is important that before any further discussions take place, a contract is drawn up between not only the team and the manager but also between the team members. You will remember the importance of contracting in coaching. It is as important in teams! How are you all going to work together? What are acceptable and unacceptable behaviours? How is the manager going to work with the team? Expectations? The coaching manager will not only contract with each individual they will also contract with the team. Some teams actually draw up a formal written contract outlining what they are going to achieve, how they are going to achieve it, and what behaviours are needed to be observed by the team members if they are going to be successful.

The first task of any coaching manager is to ensure the team know why they are a team! Each individual must know what the overall team goal is and also what specific part they will play in the quest of that goal. A coaching manager can lead a team session and outline the goals and the respective roles to the group "en masse" but they should also check on a one to one basis both in the meeting and then again with each individual outside the meeting. The second meeting is essential in order to fully check that the individual fully understands the goals and their part in the process towards hitting that goal. You would be amazed by the number of people who confirm that they fully understand what has been agreed and discussed in the meeting when actually the reality is that they don't! They are not prepared to own up in the meeting that they don't know what is happening because they do not "want to make a fool" of themselves. A good coaching manager will check understanding in the meeting and then again with individual after the meeting. Only when all the individuals in a team know the team goal and their part in supporting the team to achieve the goal will the team move forward.

So, to begin with, in summary:

- When first working with a team contract with them. How are you all going to work together?
- Identify the goal or objectives of the team.
- Work out how you are going to work together to achieve the objectives. Does the contract that you discussed still fit, or does it need adapting in order to achieve the objectives?
- Check the team's understanding of what the objectives are and then check again on an individual basis ensuring that everyone is 100% clear about what is needed to be achieved and about how it is going to be achieved. Check individual motivations as well.

These may seem simple steps but you would be amazed how many managers rush into dictating what has to be achieved without first drawing up a working contract and ensuring everyone fully understands the objectives and their specific part in the team achieving these objectives.

CHAPTER 19

Inclusion, Control and Affection

In the last chapter I discussed the importance of a successful coaching manager being able to display the same coaching behaviours in a team environment as he or she would display on a one to one basis with individuals in the team. I emphasised the fact that a coaching manager should work with individuals in relation to supporting them to identify the team goals and to contract and agree how they and the team were going to work together. It was also stressed that the coaching manager would not take for granted individuals understanding the goals and agreeing to contracts in a team setting and as such the coaching manager would always follow up such agreements on a one to one basis.

In this chapter I am going to explore an area of teams that managers are not terribly good at and that is in using the model of "inclusion", "control" and "affection" a model developed by William Shutz, an academic expert on groups.

"Inclusion" is a vital step for a team member to start to function effectively and productively in a team and without this step happening the individual concerned will not function accordingly. New members to a team must be included from the start and they must be made to feel part of the team. Many managers do not take the necessary steps to fully induct people into teams and as such many new team members take time to get functioning. In many cases, if a manager does not pro-actively take steps to ensure inclusion then the other team members may view the new team member with suspicion and distrust. How can anyone function in such an environment?

So, how does the successful coaching manager manage to include new people to the team right from the start?

Firstly, the coaching manager should have a "one to one" with the individual concerned. They should outline the aims and objectives of the team, the processes (rules, contracts, boundaries) by which the team operates and then a broad outline of the team members in terms of team roles and experience. Managers should remain silent about their own personal opinions about other team members because if they don't, there is a high chance that the manager's opinions (and perhaps prejudices) will "cloud" the new team member's opinions on future team mates. Not a healthy scenario!

Once this has happened then the coaching manager will introduce the new member to the team ensuring that beforehand he has spoken to each of the present team to inform them about the new member. The coaching manager will also ensure that perhaps a "buddy" scheme is set up whereby one team member supports the new person to "find their feet". The manager will also start to facilitate the new person's induction in the team meeting setting by asking them for their input where appropriate. This will put the new person at ease and will make them feel that not only are they being included but also that they are starting to play a role within the team right from the onset. They will start to feel valued.

I have seen too many examples over the years of where "inclusion" has not happened. I have seen managers recruit new team members and send them on initial training courses of up to six weeks duration and not make contact with them even once! I have seen managers start team meetings and not even introduce the new member and worst of all I have heard of situations where a new member was given the low down on their new team members in depth with the manager outlining who was good, who was bad, who they should mix with and who they should avoid! How comfortable did you think this new team member felt going to their first team meeting?

Whilst outlining and stressing the role of the coaching manager in team inclusion, the coaching manager should also be enabling and supporting the individual to be pro-active themselves. They should be encouraging the new team member to make early contact with the team and to make sure that they made themselves known to team mates at meetings by encouraging them to introduce themselves rather than wait for someone else to do it.

Without "inclusion" many new team members will not only fail to function effectively, they may even leave the team! Once inclusion has been achieved then the new team member can go on to the "control" and "affection" stages.

Control

After the members feel "included" within the team, then the dynamics are such that team members can start to exercise a degree of "control". By "control" I do not mean taking over the team. "Control" could mean a number of things but generally team members can exert control by simply putting their point of view across or, by airing concerns, or by putting forward proposals and suggestions. Too often, although people feel part of the team, in that they "get on well" with the manager and their team mates, people do not feel comfortable in putting across their views, whether they be ideas to move the team forward or whether it is to feedback some constructive criticism.

Sometimes this lies with the confidence of the individual team member but in my experience it generally lies with the manager taking overall control of the team and doing most of the directing. The end result of this is that talented individuals keep their ideas and views to themselves thus preventing the team for developing further.

To ensure that each member of the team is able to exert a degree of control, the coaching manager must be an excellent facilitator. They must be able to ensure that during team meetings team members have their say and are able to put their ideas and suggestions forward. In order for this to happen the coaching manager should build a "team charter" or "team agreement" whereby the team knows exactly what is expected from them in both team meeting situations and also out-with team meetings. Basically the "team charter" is a form of contract, which outlines how the team is going to operate, both in terms of process and behaviours. When everybody buys into the charter then behaviours improve and ideas, concerns and suggestions tend to come out rather than being only discussed in the "avoid at all cost" "corridor conferences". How many times have you been to a meeting where not much was said by the team during the meeting, but when people broke for a tea-break the level of noise from the team immediately rose! Usually out of earshot of the manager!

So, the successful coaching manager should facilitate the construction of a team charter and then ensure that this charter is adhered to. The coaching manager must also play their part in ensuring their meetings run effectively in that they should facilitate their meetings in that all team members get their say on each issue and that every member gets equal airtime. That means sometimes encouraging certain people to contribute more and with others, limiting the amount of airtime that they tend to use. Above all the successful coaching manager must be self-disciplined and not continually "hog the limelight"

Once you have enabled the team to exert "control" you will start to see energy levels rise and the coaching manager will always have to be prepared, as a result of this, to ensure that this energy is channelled appropriately. Do not let meetings degenerate into "dumping grounds" where all the issues and all the concerns take over the entire meeting. By all means if there are concerns then they should be aired but it is totally counter-productive for the coaching manager to start to agree with all concerns as this potentially could prevent the team from moving forward. In fact it may cause the team to go backwards. The coaching manager in this instance must facilitate and coach the team towards a productive and positive outcome. This is an area where I have seen many managers come unstuck. They have encouraged the team to be open and when they have been (particularly in areas of concern) the manager has struggled to move the team forward productively in that they have been left "hanging". By that I mean, that the team have aired their concerns and although the manager has listened, he or she has moved the conversation on and perhaps shot off at a tangent in order to avoid the concerns and to get down to "the important business". This must be avoided at all costs as it only serves to increase dissatisfaction. The successful coaching manager always facilitates and coaches the team towards a positive outcome.

So, in summary:

- ➢ Encourage "control" by facilitating the construction and implementation of a team "charter".

- ➢ Facilitate and coach the team in team meeting situations in order to encourage participation from all team members. Avoid "hogging the limelight"

- ➢ Channel the resultant increase in energy accordingly. Do not leave the team "hanging" on any issue and coach them to productive outcomes, regardless of the issues being raised.

Affection

What do we mean by affection in teams? Affection in some cases will mean love; showing warmth to; a liking towards. And perhaps this is where we start to go wrong in teams. Affection in the case of teams means simply that we appreciate the contribution of others. It doesn't mean that we have to agree with what others in the team are saying, but what we should appreciate is the fact that they are contributing both in terms of effort and input of ideas. Too often we are too quick to discount people's inputs and contributions because we have our own ideas or that, perhaps we haven't listened fully to what people have to say.

Once someone is "included" in a team, and then they are able to have a degree of "control" they must be given some "affection". This "affection" may only take the form of listening to ideas and it may only take the form of two words - thank-you. But these two words are probably the most powerful form of motivational feedback there is!

If you consider the analogy that the model of Inclusion, Control and Affection is the equivalent of the foundations, structure and cement of a building then we can start to see why each part of the ICA model is important. Consider, the building. You must have strong foundations. The equivalent of this in a team is the need to ensure everyone is included. Without the team members being included, the result is that they feel isolated and tend to withdraw and their input is lessened thus the team suffers. In a building if you have shaky foundations then the whole structure is put at risk of collapse.

In a building once you have a sound foundation, you have to make sure that the supporting structure, in terms if the walls and roof is sound. In a team, the structure must be there in terms of the people and the people not only have to be included, they need to have some control. Imagine a building with an insecure wall or roof. How often have you heard the term, "the roof caved in"? The same can be applied to teams. Without giving people some form of control, you may have the foundations of a team, but your whole structure will be very shaky unless you give people the strength by giving them some control.

Finally, in a building once your foundations are laid and you put up the supporting structure, you have to secure that structure by the use of cement, nails and screws. You can do similar with a team by ensuring that affection takes place. Listen to people's contributions. Thank them for them. They may not always be taken up but at least people will say, "I was given a good hearing". Always thank people for the efforts that they put in. This is the cement and nails that keeps a team together.

In summary;

- Include everyone from the start. Make them feel welcome and ensure that each team member includes everyone else.

- Ensure that everyone in the team exhibits a degree of "control" in that they feel comfortable inputting their ideas and contributions.

- Show "affection" by thanking each person for his or her effort and contributions and ideas. Encourage the individuals in the team to do likewise. A coaching manager will lead the way but will also encourage participation from each individual.

CHAPTER 20

Stages of Team Development

One of the greatest challenges a coaching manager has is in moving his or her team though the various team development stages. If a manager has no, or little experience of teams and team dynamics then taking over a team and then leading that team can be a very stressful experience. Every manager should know what the various growth stages are of a developing team and they should know how best to move the team through these stages with the minimum of fuss and stress. Unfortunately, many managers do not get the necessary training or coaching in this area of team development and as such teams go through a lot of stress and turmoil when perhaps this could be minimised quite considerably.

In the next couple of pages I will take you through a simple team development model, which I find the most useful of all the models I have studied. The names of each of the stages sum up perfectly what you can expect at each stage!

Psychologist, B.W Tuckman in the 1970s, developed this model and Tuckman suggests that there are four team development stages that teams have to go through to be productive. The four stages are:

➤　　　*Forming* when the team meets and starts to work

together for the first time.
➤   Storming, when the members within the team start to "jockey" for position and when control struggles take place.
➤   Norming when rules are finalised and accepted and when team rules start being adhered to.
➤   Performing when the team starts to produce through effective and efficient working practices.

Some teams will go through the four stages fairly rapidly and move from forming through to performing in a relatively short space of time. A lot depends on the composition of the team, the capabilities of the individuals, the tasks at hand, and of course the leadership from management. One thing is certain – no team passes over the storming phase. All teams must be prepared to go through the difficult and stressful times as well as reaping the benefits of the productive phases. The task of the coaching manager is to identify where along the path of team development his or her team is and then move it on to the next phase with the minimum of fuss and resistance.

Let's look at each of the stages in detail.

Forming

This is a stressful phase when new teams come together. Everyone is a bit wary of each other, particularly if they do not know anyone and particularly if the manager is new. Even more stressful, if the rumours circulating about the manager are not favourable!

The first meeting is a nervous one and a good coaching manager will recognise this and make attempts to ensure the team is put at ease. As the forming stage is the stage where cliques can develop, the coaching manager should be aware of this and should be aware of the various alliances that will occur at this stage. Not all alliances will be counter-productive to the team's future success but it pays for the coaching manager to watch and observe the behaviours of potential cliques. The challenge for the coaching manager is basically to give an inert group of people who hardly know each the best start possible as a new team. The coaching manager should attempt to do the following to give the team the best possible start.

- Outline specifically the task the team has to perform.
- Be specific about each person's role in the team's task.
- Outline how the team has come together and give reasons as to why the various team members have been brought together for inclusion within this team.
- Be open about the way you operate as a manager - what are your strengths and weaknesses? Outline your expectations of both the team and the individuals within the team. In other words, start to contract with the team.
- Encourage each team member to do likewise.
- Ensure that the team has a set of rules and guidelines and that the team has an input into how these rules are formed and agreed.
- Have a discussion about reward and recognition. How does the team want to celebrate its achievements?
- How are the team going to make decisions?
- How are the team going to give feedback on each other's performance?

By having an open discussion right at the start of the team's task then people get the chance to air views, concerns and queries. The coaching manager will enable this to happen with the result that people feel they have been listened to; they have been able to contribute; they know the rules and regulations by which the team will operate and they now have a greater appreciation of the people they are working with.

Storming

Storming is a challenging phase and the coaching manager who has led the team through the forming stage well and is starting to feel quite good about progress may have quite a rude awakening. Storming always seems to come as a surprise, no matter how well the coaching manager has prepared and led the team up till now. This is where the leadership qualities of the coaching manager are tested to the full. I have had the privilege of working with some managers who have handled this stage well and also have witnessed (and suffered) at the hands of managers who have had no idea of what to do to move the team forward.

Storming usually arises as a result of goals, roles and rules all becoming confused and unclear. No matter how clear the team was in relation to the goals, roles and rules during the forming stage it is very often the case that the individual team member interpretations of these roles and rules is somewhat different in reality. This results in confusion when different behaviours are evident and conflicts can arise with the potential for factions being created within the team.

It is during this stage that the coaching skills of the coaching manager should come to the fore. Both individuals and the team as a whole should be coached to enable and support them to ensure agreement as regards what specifically the goals, roles and rules are with respect to the team and what that means to each and every individual. Many managers get frustrated at this stage because they believe that they have already done the work at outlining the goals, roles and rules at the early stage of the formation of the team. I have seen managers go from a state of immense pride about the way they have guided their team through the early stages to a state of anger where they look to blame the team and its individual members. What is it they say, "Comes before a fall"?

The successful coaching manager must go over again the agreements made by the team during the forming stage and ensure that the understanding is uniform across the team. The earlier in the storming stage this is revisited the better and this is where the aware coaching manager comes into his or her own. The unaware manager will tend to panic and blame and will be unable to control the behaviours of the team even though they may take a very authoritarian stance and start to order that people behave. All that achieves is compliance and team members will still have the same misunderstandings about what is going on. This is when a lot of talking goes on "behind the manager's back" This is very unhealthy for a team.

Once the coaching manager has got his or her team through the storming phase they have to be aware of a challenge that can come out of the blue. And that is the challenge of a new member. No sooner has a coaching manager got their team through the "storm" then it is joined by a new member who then starts to question the ways of working and potentially starts to destabilise the team. All new members to the team must be made aware of the team goals, roles and rules before they join and they must be made aware of the process that is in place or the giving and receiving of feedback if they have any suggestions as to how they can improve the ways of working for the team. Again, this is an area where I have seen managers lose the progress that they have made with their team. Instead of taking time out to bring a new member up to speed with all the rules, roles and goals, the manager lets the new member join the team without much of a briefing. The result can be chaos. Beware.

You will find at times that there will be people who tend to hold back the storming process or perhaps prolong it. These people have a decision to make. Go with the majority or get out. Business has no place to let the odd individual hold things up. That may seem tough coming from a "coaching" manager but this is reality and in many cases management is a tough role. This is one of these instances.

Norming

Do you remember what it is like when a real storm passes? The winds drop, the sky brightens, the birds sing again. Teamwork is like this also. There is a calm, a focus. Goals are clearly understood. Roles are clarified. The rules and regulations are being adhered to and people are working together positively. Relationships become stronger as people are more aware of each other. Strengths and weaknesses are realised and utilised accordingly. Norming is characterised by acceptance. Whereas in the storming stage, people were apt to rebel very quickly, this is now not the case and if someone has a grievance, complaint or suggestion then the proper processes are used and people tend to be listened to. The role of the coaching manager in this stage is to ensure that this calm continues and that any behaviours that arise that may threaten the calm are channelled in the right direction. Also the coaching manager has an important role in conveying information particularly in relation to the successes that are starting to occur within the team. The coaching manager should be spending a lot of time with individual team members coaching them and supporting them to develop their capabilities that relate to the individual's team role and the tasks that they have to perform in relation to the team goals.

Performing

Not every team makes it to the performing stage. Many get stuck at Norming and although everything appears normal, there is a lack of momentum and motivation towards achieving the all important team goals. It is as though the team is comfortable in this stage and does not want to progress further for fear of returning to a storming stage, a stage that probably was very uncomfortable for most people.

It is at the performing stage where team members really concentrate on the team goals. They are determined to work towards them, as they know what rewards are available to them on completion. They are also aware of the strengths and weaknesses of the team, and they appreciate these, and also works towards developing the weaknesses. This is a period of great personal growth among team members. There is a good deal of sharing of experiences, feelings and ideas together with the development of a fierce loyalty towards team members. There will be arguments, disagreements and disputes but these will be facilitated positively as the team will now live and die by its rules. The coaching manager at this stage will play very much a non-directive role, concentrating on strategy to plan the next way forward. The team will be in many ways, self-directing, perhaps even self-appraising with the manager taking very much a back-seat role. Again the manager's role will be to facilitate communication and ensure that the successes are communicated and rewarded.

In summary

> *Forming.* The successful coaching manager will ensure that the team meets and understands the team goals, the roles they have to take on and the rules by which they have to play. The coaching manager will realise that although there may be a great deal of agreement and compliance about what is discussed many people will have different interpretations of what is agreed. One to ones help but inevitably there will start to be undercurrents of disagreement as to what has exactly been agreed.

➤ *Storming.* Once the disagreements and blame start, get the team quickly together to thrash out what the concerns and disagreements are. The coaching manager at this stage is strong, directive but also fair. The team needs direction at this stage and perhaps people need to hear things that perhaps they don't want to hear. Get things out in the open. Let the team bleed a little and then begin the healing process by facilitating their coming together.

➤ *Norming.* Lessen the direction and spend time with individuals starting to coach them in relation to their roles within the team and the tasks that they have to perform. At the same time the coaching manager will be challenging team members to take on extra capabilities to move the team on to the next stage.

➤ *Performing.* Take a step back and allow the team to become self-directing. Be there for them and continue your coaching role with both team and individuals. Allow individuals to take on leadership roles and encourage rotation of roles. Communicate success and reward success accordingly.

CHAPTER 21

Rules and Regulations

Many people immediately "turn off" when one talks about teams having rules and regulations. I remember many years ago when I first introduced "ground rules" for behaviours in meetings, the looks that I got and the initial "disgruntlement" that was evident. "We don't need ground-rules. We operate as a team already and we are all grown adults!" was one immediate reply. I backed off and let them proceed with the meeting. What a shambles! No agenda, no chairperson, people talking over each other, subgroups forming and a lot, lot more. Not only did the group need proper facilitation they needed to be aware of what behaviours were not acceptable and what behaviours were desired. There eventually was agreement that this team's state of affairs was unacceptable.

So, what can the coaching manager do with their teams to ensure that not only meetings go smoothly and productively but also general behaviours are positive and constructive? Ground-rules are important as they give people a framework to work productively behind. People need to know what is acceptable and what is not and once they know where they stand they will start to abide by them. Ground rules also provide a framework for the giving and receiving of feedback so when someone follows the rules explicitly they should be congratulated and praised and when someone transgresses or flouts the rules the opposite will apply. That person will be informed of the impact that their negative behaviours are having on the group and its productivity.

A coaching manager will ensure that the team forms the ground rules themselves. Too often I have seen managers impose their "rules" on the team and as such there has been little acceptance of them. This behaviour from a manager is seen as dictatorial and is usually borne out of fear. The "do as I say" set of rules are not very productive. Get the team to discuss what behaviours they feel uncomfortable with within the team and what behaviours they feel will drive the team forward productively. Let them come up with a list and let them produce what in some instances is called the team "charter". If there are some "givens" then make sure you outline them right from the start, as most organisations will have various processes that must be adhered to. For example, for a sales rep, it may be that call records must be filled in after each sales call and sent off to Head Office that following evening. Get the "givens" out of the road and then facilitate and coach the team to come up with their own set of ground rules. If they have input to these then they are far more likely to adhere to them and to give feedback to individuals when the rules are flouted or ignored.

In the short term as constructive feedback on negative behaviours is difficult for most people the coaching manager will have to take the lead, and lead by example. If a manager is seen to ignore the rules or ignore giving feedback to someone who does not abide by the rules then other team members start to wonder what the point is!

In summary:

➤ Ground rules may seem too formal but they are very important if a team is to function properly and productively.

➤ The coaching manager should let the team form their own set of ground rules but only after the company "givens" are discussed and agreed to.

➤ The coaching manager does not dictate the rules but plays the coach and facilitates the team to come up with their own set of agreed rules.

➤ The coaching manager will lead by example and give feedback when both the rules are adhered too well and also when they are ignored.

CHAPTER 22

Team Meetings

Managers spend probably too much time in meetings but meetings can also be a fantastic medium in which to coach and develop the team. Provided the meeting is for a useful purpose (and amazingly a good number are not!) then the manager can use this opportunity to use their coaching skills to great effect. The following are some pointers as to how you, as a manager, can make the most productive use of team meetings.

1. Why are you calling the meeting? Make sure it is for a distinct purpose with measurable objectives and outcomes. There is nothing worse than calling a meeting with little substance just because it is the norm. I have been to many sales review meetings, which were held every month because that it what has always been done. Only call the meeting if it is necessary!

2. As a manager you will have outcomes based on your agenda items but will they take up the whole time? Ask the team what they would like to see on the agenda and get people to take responsibility for running their particular session or topic. Make sure they have practical outcomes.

3. Once the agenda is compiled make sure that each agenda

item has a desired outcome and that this outcome will be achieved through an agreed process. It helps to vary the process for different agenda items where possible. Use presentation. group discussion, role-play etc to make meetings varied and enjoyable. Sitting through a day meeting where the manager hogs the stage and presents back all the time does not make for a productive meeting!

4. Communicate the agenda outlining to the team what topics are to be discussed, what process is to be used and what the outcomes are for each topic. If there is any preparation work to be done ensure that each individual knows what they have to do and what they have to bring with them. Ensure each agenda topic has a timescale and it is probably best to prioritize the topics in relation to importance and urgency to the business.

5. Before the meeting starts remind people the "ground rules" that you have, as a team, put in place for meetings. Also it useful to have a minute or actions taker and a timekeeper so as to help the meeting process go smoothly.

6. Check the "mood" of the team before the meeting takes place. Has anything cropped up that may have an affect of the group and hence the previously agreed agenda? If the group's minds are elsewhere then you may not achieve your meeting's outcomes. I remember a sales meeting many years ago where the manager insisted that we go through the agreed agenda (his!) despite the fact that the company only the day before had issued a profits warning and that there may be redundancies. Was anyone really interested at that point in time about last month's sales report! No! Flex your agenda to address fears and concerns first before moving on.

7. Ensure participation from each individual where appropriate. It is important that all team members feel "included", that they have a degree of "control" and that people are thanked for their contributions ("affection"). Again remind yourself of the ICA model of teams by referring to a previous chapter.

8. Continually check the process and mood of the group. Is the process working for them and is the meeting on track to achieve its aims? If not, be flexible; adapt either the process or agenda or both.

9. Make sure there are adequate breaks for teas/coffees/lunch. Do not try to cram an agenda.

10. Where possible, build in development time for the group. Can you use some meeting time to deliver aspects of your training plan or development plan for the team. People feel great if they leave meetings having fulfilled their agenda outcomes and also learned something new that they can take back to their roles.

11. On the development side ensure you give people the chance to develop their meeting skills such as meeting organisation, coaching and facilitation. As the manager do you always have to organise and run the meeting? No - develop your team's individuals to take on such tasks periodically! And make sure you coach and direct them appropriately when they take on such developmental tasks so as to give them the necessary support to deliver. Do not dump the tasks on them without giving them support. Otherwise your meeting may not go, as you would have hoped!

12. Make sure all the main discussion points and actions are

documented and circulated so as you can follow up on
progress with each topic.

13.   Get feedback from the team as to how the meeting went and
         how it was for them. Did you achieve the meeting's objectives?
         What went well? What not so well? What do you have to do
         next time in order to make your next meeting even better?

Meetings are a chance for you as a manager, to communicate to,
listen to, inspire and develop your team and the individuals. Although
not all meetings called can achieve this, if you as a manager are in
control you can ensure that your meetings go well and that people
look forward to them if you follow the above principles.

CHAPTER 23

Dealing with Disruptives

As the successful coaching manager takes an "open" stance to team meetings in that he or she will encourage greater participation, commitment and responsibility there are some team members who may take advantage of this increased openness. In this chapter I will outline some types of individuals who may have to be handled correctly in order for team conflict to be minimised.

The "Prima Donna"

These people tend to be very talented and also tend to let people know about it! They think that because of their talent they do not have to abide by the team's agreed rules and they demand that the other team members attend to them, while they themselves ignore the needs of the team. Even when the team do try to include the "prima donna" they are brushed off. The "prima donna" oozes arrogance. How does the coaching manager handle this type of person?

Firstly recognise that their personality is not their fault and secondly appreciate that what you see is not all there is. Arrogant people often have major insecurities and may actually be experiencing more pain and stress than other team members. There may also be stresses out with the workplace so be prepared to perhaps at some point to become the "counselling" manager or if you are not qualified in that area, to refer onwards. Thirdly, just check that the team itself is not causing the problem. Sometimes the "prima donna's" arrogance is due to being excluded from the team as the team find it hard to deal with the "Prima Donna's" extra talent and to that end start to exclude them deliberately. Also check that your team rules are not so strict that they are preventing creativity and innovation.

The behaviour of the "Prima Donna" must be highlighted to the "Prima Donna" themselves and a coaching manager will ensure that not only is the feedback given constructively but also a "listening ear" is given as to why the behaviour is occurring. Only then can a meaningful discussion take place as to how best to move forward in order that the disruptive behaviours are replaced with productive ones along with the scope for the "Prima Donna" to remain at their creative best. It may be useful to consider giving them a "specialist" role within the team and make sure that you keep reviewing their progress with them regularly and don't forget the recognition of their efforts!

The "Dominator"

Every team has them – a person who always wants to dominate team activities and ensure they get the lion share of attention. The usual way of dealing with the dominator is to "slap them down" by either telling them outright to quit their domineering behaviours or by both ignoring and talking over them or by relegating them to tasks out with the team. I believe this is counter-productive and it is in these situations where the coaching manager comes to the fore in team meetings. How about the following:

a. Call on the other team members to contribute. When the "dominator" pipes up acknowledge their contribution and encourage the other team members to come up with their own contributions.

b. Make the team agenda work by sticking to it. Many "dominators" will throw in "wobblies" that take the team away from the agenda. As the coaching manager, ensure tangents do not happen and bring the meeting back on course.

c.   When the "dominator" throws in an idea or a suggestion then probe as to what is behind the suggestion, how it fits with the agenda and desired outcomes of the topic or meeting, and then asks the team for their comments and thoughts on it. Don't agree with the dominator before the other contributions!

d.   If the "dominator" continues to attempt to control the meeting, than at the next break take them aside and give them the constructive feedback that they deserve! They must be told of the negative impact of their interventions.

The "You Owe Me" Individuals

These people think that the company they work for owes them in terms of a job, a decent wage and good working conditions. In many ways they act like "spoilt brats" and expect everything to be done for them. They take a very negative approach and will complain at the slightest change in company policy. Examples include the company car policy, lunch allowances, pensions, entertainment budgets and holiday entitlements. This has resulted in many cases due to people becoming too comfortable as a result of reduced responsibility. In other words it is due to bad or mediocre performance management by managers themselves!

The coaching manager can handle the "you owe mes" through vigilance and intolerance. Vigilance, in terms of closely monitoring performance against agreed performance objectives and intolerance in terms of ensuring that these objectives are not so easily achievable that the person is not stretched. Too often team members get by by doing the minimum when really they should have to work to hit objectives. Only by having stretching objectives will they ever perform at the highest level. Rewards that are given must be for achievement and not for simply "turning up".

The "Saboteur"

There will be on occasion times when you as a coaching manager will have to deal with the "saboteur". This is the team member who tells you one thing and then does another. Or, tells the team one thing and then tells you another. They are out to split the team and perhaps create a division between the manager and the rest of the team. Sometimes they can pick on individuals. Perhaps they see them as a threat and as such start to spread rumours about them, or worse, sneak to the boss to tell them when the person has made a mistake. Even worse than that is to tell lies about them or about what they have done!

There is only one way to deal with "saboteurs". Firstly establish exactly what the truth is. Once this is established and that you are 100% certain in your facts, and that you have found out that the "saboteur" has been at work, then confront them and start the disciplinary process. Sounds harsh? It is and deserves to be. Teams cannot sustain saboteurs and the saboteur has to know how destructive their behaviours are and they also have to now what the consequences of their behaviours are in relation to the team. This sort of behaviour cannot be tolerated!

CHAPTER 24

Balancing the Mix

With regards to teams the coaching manager will always where possible try to get the right mix of both personalities and skills within the team. Many times this is not possible, especially where a manager takes on a team that is already formed. In this case the coaching manager has a challenge whereby if there are any gaps in either personality or skills he or she must endeavour to fill these gaps. I have found two models useful in assessing the mix of the team. Firstly there is the behavioural styles model, which is covered, in an earlier chapter and secondly there is the Belbin Model of Team Roles.

If we first look at Behavioural Styles, ideally you would want to have a team that was a mixture of all four styles. i.e. Driver to add focus and assertion; Analyst to add method, structure and quality, Expressive to add creativity, energy and innovation and Amiable to add diplomacy and harmony. An imbalance can lead to the coaching manager having to firstly identify the gap and then fill the gap by adapting his or her own behavioural style in order to reinstate the balance. Looking at extremes. If you a team of four individuals and each individual had the same behavioural style you might experience the following:

All Drivers
You would certainly get focus and a drive to get results. However

given that drivers usually think that their way is best, you may get conflict as people try to get their own way. Also there may be a lack of creativity and quality about their work.

All Analysts

Plenty of quality and structure here but again a lack of creativity and energy may mean that the task takes ages to be completed, if at all!

All Amiable

Loads of harmony and together-ness with a degree of creativity although this group will always look for reassurance and support. They will need to ask for advice and opinions from senior management. Distinct lack of risk taking and again may take far too long to complete the task.

All Expressive

Loads of energy, ideas and risks but little structure, quality and method. Error prone and may end up completing projects but with the wrong result!

Getting the right balance of styles can pay big dividends if your are looking for the team to function well but the coaching manager will have to be a good facilitator and coach as having the right mix means different styles working together and there is always the tendency for the styles to clash.

Another model, which is useful, is Meredith Belbin's Team Roles Model, an outline of which is given below.

BELBIN'S TEAM ROLES (adapted from Belbin, 1981)

Role	Observed contributions
Chairperson	1. Clarifying the goals and objectives of the group. 2. Selecting the problems on which decisions have to be made, and establishing their priorities. 3. Helping establish roles, responsibilities and work boundaries within the group. 4. Summing up the feelings and achievements of the group, and articulating group verdicts.
Shaper	1. Shaping roles, boundaries, responsibilities, tasks and objectives. 2. Finding or seeking to find pattern m group discussion. 3. Pushing the group towards agreement on policy and action and towards making decisions.
Plant	1. Advancing proposals. 2. Making criticisms that lead up to counter-suggestions. 3. Offering new insights on lines of action already agreed.
Monitor / evaluator	1. Analysing problems and situations. 2. Interpreting complex written material and clarifying obscurities. 3. Assessing the judgements and contributions of others.
Company worker	1. Transforming talk and ideas into practical steps. 2. Considering what is feasible. 3. Trimming suggestions to make them fit into agreed plans and established systems.
Team worker	1. Giving personal support and help to others. 2. Building on to or seconding a member's ideas and suggestions. 3. Drawing the reticent into discussion. 4. Taking steps to avert or overcome disruption of the team
Resource investigator	1. Introducing ideas and developments of external origin.

	2. Contacting other individuals or groups of own volition.
	3. Engaging in negotiation-type activities.
Completer	1. Emphasizing the need for task completion, meeting W" and schedules and generally promoting a sense of urgency.
	2. Looking for and spotting errors, omissions and oversights.
	3. Galvanizing others into activity.

By utilising the models above the coaching manager can help raise awareness of the team's strengths and weaknesses and ensure that the right approach is taking to developing the team further.

CHAPTER 25

The Successful Coaching Manager as Facilitator

One of the most beneficial skills sets a coaching manager can have is that of facilitation. This is not a skill that one can pick up overnight and certainly not from a book of this size and magnitude. However perhaps I can start the process of you wanting to know and learn more about facilitation by outlining some of the key aims that facilitators have. These are:

> - to actively involve all members of a group in decision-making.
> - to maximise individuals' commitment and engagement.
> - to build a team spirit that lasts.
> - to achieve consensus.
> - to articulate a shared vision.
> - to make plans that really happen.

Below are some criteria for facilitator excellence as stated by John Heron, a leading expert in the field of facilitation. How do you stack up as a coaching manager in this respect?

1. **Authority** You have "distress-free" authority and do not carry your personal emotional or organisational "baggage"

through your interventions with the team.

2.   **Confrontation** You can confront supportively, and work effectively on unaware intrusions and other defensive forms within the groups. In other words you are able to challenge unproductive behaviours so that a favourable outcome is achieved despite the intrusion.

3.   **Orientation** You can provide clear, conceptual orientation as appropriate, in and among experiential work. Another way of saying you can let the group know where they are exactly are in relation to their goal at any given point in time.

4.   **Care** You come over to groups as caring, empathetic, warm and genuine. How many managers can say this?

5.   **Range of Methods** You can use and access a good number of models of personal and team development that will enable the group to grow and move forward.

6.   **Respect of Persons** You can, in practice, respect fully the autonomy of the persons involved in the group or team and the right of them to change and grow.

7.   **Flexibility of Style** You can move deftly and flexibly, as every situation needs, between group dynamics and also adapt your personal style to that of the individual members of the group or team.

Many managers become proficient at coaching one to one but start to struggle when confronted with the team. By becoming a good facilitator of groups and teams the coaching manager can move their team to far greater heights of performance.

CHAPTER 26

Ensuring Reward & Recognition

As we discussed earlier in this book, reward and recognition is vital if people are to remain motivated. The same goes for teams but how can you reward a team of people so that each and every team member is motivated?

Teams as a whole are not motivated by "blanket" schemes such a cash bonuses or holidays. Such schemes particularly where money has to be divided up based on contribution and/or success can be downright destructive if mis-handled. And do all team members want to go on that super four-day trip to Dubai? Don't think so!

If, you as a coaching manager are going to reward and recognise your team for their efforts and success why not consider the following:

➤ Make the next team meeting a good one at a good venue such as a top class hotel with leisure facilities. Throw is some leisure time such as a round of golf or a massage.

➤ Get the team members involved in the formation and running of the meeting so that it is their meeting with the manager having only a "slot"

➤ Run some simple competitions whereby the team

votes for individuals within the team. E.g. "Most Improved performer"

➤ Run a team newsletter where successes are listed and perhaps individuals interviewed on specific project work.

➤ Give the team a slice of your budget to work with in relation to project work or setting up the motivational meeting.

➤ Use some of your budget to perhaps upgrade equipment such as the latest laptop or projector.

➤ How about a free lunch or dinner for them and their spouses? Concert tickets?

➤ Talk to them! As a team tell them how much you value their expertise and effort. Tell them as a team and as individuals!

These are just simple things you can do to thank and motivate a team as a whole but it is not as plain sailing as this. Sometimes there will be distinct differences in performance on a team objective or project and to ensure that everyone is rewarded according to their performance the coaching manager will have to ensure that they oversee reward schemes that make sure that performance is taken into account, especially where money is at stake!

If you are considering a reward scheme that involves bonus money then how do you go about ensuring a fair distribution of that money based on performance? And who makes the decisions? You as the manager? Or do you let the team decide? Consider the following before proceeding:

➤ The scheme must be simple to understand and simple to monitor and calculate.

➤ Everyone must fully understand what he or she needs to do to make the scheme work for him or her.

➤   Updates must be regular and a mechanism for queries must be put in place.

Rewarding a team of individuals can be very complex given the different styles, personalities and needs involved but with a little dedicated time and input from the team, good reward schemes and initiatives can be produced which will help to ensure that the team gets the recognition they deserve.

PART III

Articles Relating to Coaching within Management

The following articles have been published or have been submitted for publishing within several websites and magazines.

The Top 10 Essentials when implementing a productive corporate coaching programme

1. **Ensure that you have fully studied the commercial impact of having a coaching culture**

   Selling the concept to the Board and senior management can be a tough process. Make sure you are prepared with a good case for the organisation to implement this change programme. Ensure that you have passion and belief in what you are selling to them and that you have the commercial evidence available that implementing such a programme will mean increased commercial gain.

2. **Identify the key stakeholders and make sure that they buy-in to the fact that a coaching culture makes economic sense for the organisation**

   Make sure you identify the correct decision makers within the organisation. You will need to ensure they understand exactly what coaching is, what it entails and what it can bring to the business. They will need to see evidence of results and outcomes together with projections of costs and any downturn in productivity while the change is being implemented.

3. **Encourage the CEO and key stakeholders to "walk their talk" and make public their support of the coaching culture**

   Once you have their buy-in, you must ensure that they start to implement the coaching strategy themselves and that their talk and behaviours reflect this. There is nothing worse that a Board who talk a good game and then play a completely different one. It is very de-motivational for employees if they see that the senior management do not support the initiative.

4. **Don't try to implement the programme for change overnight and for everyone. Identify a pilot group**

Do not try to implement this overnight. Plan it out over months and years rather than weeks. The length of time will depend on the size of your organisation and also on how deeply entrenched the organisation is in terms of a particular culture. Start by identifying a group or department where feel the coaching culture will take off. Don't try and use a problem department!

5. **Identify key roles or individuals who will ensure effective implementation**

You may want to consider creating a new role to implement the culture. Your organisation may have the resources to bring in outside consultants but what is vital is that you have "champions" within the organisation itself who are committed to ensuring effective change. Such roles tend to be coaching roles and in some cases they are known as "change agents".

6. **Train the "coaches" in coaching before letting them loose!**

If you identify particular staff from within the organisation to take on these coach or "change agent" roles make sure you recruit well and that you train them adequately before they begin the process of change. Inadequately trained coaches can cause more demotivation than motivation!

7. **Communicate the progress of the pilot – Good and not so good!**

It is vital that the rest of the organisation is kept up to date with progress. Results and employee feedback should be communicated as often as is possible and avoid at all costs the "happy" feedback where "everything in the garden is rosy". It won't be! It is better to communicate both the good results and the not so good. It is also essential to communicate reasons as to why things are working and not working together with, in the case of things not working, an alternative plan to make them work.

8.   **Link the changes in behaviour/culture to any increases in productivity and/or employee morale**
The Board and Senior Management will want to see outcomes and it is essential that you link any changes in behaviour and/or practice to the results obtained. Manage their expectations carefully.

9.   **Keep training the "coaches". Their development should belonging and not a one-off**
Make sure your coaches and "change agents" have ongoing development. Coaches do not become effective overnight and a one off programme will not ensure they are capable of maintaining the change process. Their development plans should be ongoing and they, themselves, have some form of external coaching support.

10.   **Give this project time**
Plan this programme over years and not months. You may see a downturn in productivity to begin with but if you stick with it, manage your stakeholders, continually support your key staff, and link all initiatives to results then watch future employee morale soar and profits follow!

Why the Internal Company Coach has to be strong!

I write this article having just left twenty years of corporate life in the pharmaceutical industry, the last six years being that of an internal corporate coach. I have decided to set up my own coaching business because (a) I wanted to be free and to decide and have control over my own and my family's future, and (b) to be in a stronger position to support both managers to become better coaches and to support internal corporate coaches to become as "powerful" and recognised as they should be.

My own experience as an internal coach is that at present the ability of managers to coach effectively is not what it should be and that those people who have become internal coaches are being held back from becoming the effective coaches they should really be if organisations are to realise the potential of their people.

Why do I say this?

I became an internal coach after having been a sales executive and sales manager. The people I then had to work with found difficulty in accepting what specifically a coach was and as a result how a coach could support them. Coaching was for "people who needed help" and as such many people didn't want to be seen to use the services of the coach. Managers in authority certainly did not accept challenge from someone who was "below" them in terms of seniority or grading. Coaches were there to do the senior managers' "bidding" and as a result those coaches that did the "bidding", did not build any trust with the other employees they were meant to be coaching. Some coaches, (and it was aimed at me on one occasion) were the manager's "right hand man", a person not to trust!

The biggest challenge I found as an internal coach was being pressurised to divulge information that a coachee had confidentially confided to me. I remember on a number of occasions, incurring the wrath of my manager, when I refused to answer questions about a particular employee. This was extremely difficult for me to do; as I had always been brought up to respect authority and when your boss said jump.... You jumped! It was painful, but I stuck to my guns.

The upside of this was, that although the manager became angry with you, the employees began to trust you and I had some really fantastic coaching sessions with people after that.

Eventually, as I became a more confident coach (thanks to my own external coach) I became more comfortable challenging senior managers' behaviours and when they realised that this was for their own good, I began to see some real behavioural changes in managers, so much so, that today when I look at some of these managers, I see managers that are now actually quite good coaches!

My advice to any internal corporate coach, who has been selected from other roles, is to ensure that at the onset, you make time to ensure that you contract your coaching role. Sit down with your manager, your team, any other employees that you will be coaching, and ensure that they realise what coaching is all about, how a coach operates, what your expectations are (check theirs!) and how coaching can benefit them personally. Make sure you manage the "authority bit" and be brave in terms of challenging higher authority behaviours where they need challenging.

Another piece of advice is to ensure that your development is ongoing. I was thrown into coaching at a time of extreme organisational change and miracles were expected overnight. "You're the coach - sort it out" was heard on numerous occasions - and this, only weeks in the role. I was lucky, though, to have my own coach. He was an external coach and did not pull any punches, both with my behaviours and me and also with some of my colleagues and superiors. I can honestly say that some people actively avoided him because he really did challenge the wrong type of behaviour. But he was also so supportive in these challenges and I found that the more I worked with him, the more confident I became in not only my skills, but also myself. He really did change the way I looked at my life and myself.

You can only have an external coach for so long (budgets etc) although I would advise that the internal coach sets up supportive networks for themselves. These may be internal (I was part of an Action Learning Set - and it proved invaluable) or with other coaches externally - get involved in both. They are a great way of learning and will be there when you need support. Also, ensure that you yourself have a personal development plan, and ensure you stick to it. As a coach, if you are preaching personal development, then you have to show leadership and lead by example.

All in all, the internal coach can be a very powerful development resource for an organisation. The selected person has to be strong, have character, and be able to deal with the culture clashes, the personalities, the politics and they will have to work hard initially to contract their coaching role so as everybody, regardless of status, knows specifically what a coach does, what a coach can do for them, and how a coach operates.

Be strong, be successful, and see yourself and your coachees grow!

"The Coaching Cascade" – Myth or Reality?

There is still a mindset, particularly in the older business person, that in order to get to the top, one must be seen to "do it oneself". "You must be tough, pro-active and use your authority where necessary" was one older businessman's words of wisdom to me when I interviewed him about why he had managed to get to the top of his organisation. On asking him how he was viewed by his peers and the people who worked for him he replied: "They are probably a bit scared of me – after all I can hire and fire. There are a few who challenge me but normally I get my way."

How prevalent is this attitude in business today? I would suggest it is definitely on the wane. More and more Chief Executives and Senior Managers are waking up to the fact that using their authority is not always the best way to motivate and develop their reports. There is mounting evidence that taking a coaching approach is the more effective way forward in ensuring employees are motivated, capable and productive. I would suggest though, that there is a long, long way to go in terms of ensuring that coaching happens at all levels in an organisation. My research of several top businesses in Scotland has indicated a trend, a trend, which, although positive, seems to have ground to a bit of a halt. Let me explain.

Executive Coaching in Scotland is starting to happen. It is certainly happening at CEO and Managing Director level. These guys are paying "big bucks" for it too! The plan is then for these very same CEOs and Managing Directors to cascade this coaching down the organisational hierarchy. The CEO will have their own personal coach and as the CEOs coaching skills develop, the CEO will coach the Senior Manager who will then coach the middle manager and so on. But it appears to be coming to a grinding halt after the CEO! Why?

I asked a senior manager if he would take me on as his coach. He replied. "I am totally bought into the concept of coaching and I can see how you can support me. I have however a mentor in my CEO". "How well does he coach you?" I asked. There was silence for a while. "I get great advice and I respect his experience". So, the CEO gets an external coach, pays "big bucks" for them, and then becomes a mentor! Giving advice is great when it is great advice but what happens to new ideas and does giving advice restrict the risk taking that businesses need to in order to grow?

Why do CEOs and Managing Directors in addition to giving great advice not become great coaches? Do they not have the coaching capability or does the old ego get in the way? Probably a mixture of both. Also, how capable is the coach of the CEO in developing the CEOs coaching capability?

How can the Senior Manager then cascade the coaching philosophy and capability to his or her reports if what they are experience from on high is mentorship as opposed to real effective coaching? Coaching has to happen at all levels if an organisation is to realise the potential of all its employees. Coaching cannot be stuck at the very top and although mentorship is important, coaching should be on every manager's development agenda.

So, come on CEOs and Managing Directors - stop hogging all the executive coaching! Enable all your managers to build their coaching capability by either giving them their own coach or coaching them yourselves, once you have the capability.

Allow that cascade to happen!

Don't just become a mentor, become a great coach as well!

Is Scottish Business accepting the Art of Coaching?

In sports circles, it has been accepted for years that if an athlete or sports team wants to be really successful then they need to use the services of a coach. Someone who can raise their awareness, support their aims, challenge their behaviours and actions, and someone who can support the individual or team to heighten their capabilities and produce outstanding results. Now, business too is waking up to the fact that coaching is an essential part of everyday management. But, what is the reaction in Scotland?

In America, there has been a recent "explosion" of coaches both in terms of professional "life" coaches and now "business" or "executive" coaches. This is being driven both by customer demand and the belief that the coaches have in themselves and in the power of coaching. As usual, the UK is starting to follow suit, (albeit a few years behind), particularly in the Southeast, and slowly but surely, the "ripples" are heading north.

In Scotland, there are a growing number of people becoming "life" and "business" coaches. These people tend to come from a variety of backgrounds, with life coaches coming from therapist, counsellor, psychologist and teacher backgrounds and business coaches coming from Consultancy, HR or Management.

There have been a few coaches around for years in Scotland, and many CEOs in business have had access to a coach, mainly through the large consultancies. What hasn't as yet happened is the "cascade" of coaching from Chief Executive down the company hierarchy. Why is this the case?

Why is it, that CEOs can have access to an independent coach, but the rest of the organisation can't? Some would say that it is a perk only to be had by people at the top, the people who have the most responsibility, the people who can afford it? Others would say that to have more people in the organisation having the services of a coach would be too expensive, given the charges that some "executive" coaches command. Some would even suggest that managers lower down the hierarchy don't have time to get coached and in some cases, don't deserve it! Anyway, managers never have time to coach because they are too busy doing more "important" tasks.

I have heard it said that coaching is too "soft", too "airy fairy", it is not a "hard" business skill and that it is a skill promoted by "tree huggers"! Some of these people maybe should try being coached by the coach that I had in my early days as a Business Coach. I have never been so challenged in my life, and uncomfortable as these challenges were to begin with, I found that I grew as a person and as a businessman with every coaching visit.

In my discussions with several top managers in Scottish Business, it is apparent that they are aware of coaching and in many cases, particularly the younger executives, are sold on the coaching concept and are starting to accept the fact that coaching is an excellent tool to build the capability of their staff and hence enhance company results. When asked if they themselves would lead the way and employ their own coach, many answered that they themselves had a "mentor" at the very top of the company and that they didn't need it. Is this where the coaching "cascade" is coming to a halt? The CEO or Managing Director has a coach and then he, himself becomes a mentor? (Note that he or she doesn't become a coach!) I would also suggest that having a coach might be seen by some as a "weakness" in that "I must be seen to do it myself" as opposed to "having a support". The old Scottish mindset of "being seen to be strong" raising it's ugly head again! Surely it is a sign of pro-activity and accountability to say "Hey, I have got areas I can develop and if I need someone to help me focus and get better results for my company, isn't it worth it?"

I can imagine at this stage as people are reading this, some saying "Hold on a minute, our company has dedicated coaches", or "My Managers are all trained to coach". This, I'm sure in some cases is very true, although I would go so far to suggest that in many cases, the training of managers in coaching skills is inadequate in that although managers are trained, their use of the skills are very limited when it comes down to everyday use. I would also question that going on a two day coaching course and gaining a photocopy certificate is going to make someone a great coach! My own opinion is that to become a good coach or good coaching manager you have to fully experience being coached professionally as well as knowing the theory.

How many staff, if asked, would say that their manager was a good coach? Do the staff know what good coaching is? Do they think that getting advice based on experience is good coaching? How many times has the telling of advice gone in one ear and out the other?

As regards companies who have dedicated coaches, are they real coaches or are they trainers masquerading under the name of coach? Many trainers are using the skills of coaching, and using both training and coaching skills is vital in the development of younger staff and staff employed in new positions. Coaches, on the other hand, deal with already competent people with a view to them performing excellently. Very little, if any training is needed in these situations and if a training need arises then the coach will direct them to an expert trainer in that area.

Coaching needs more and better press in Scottish Business circles than it has at present. Business needs to know exactly what coaching is, what skills are entailed, how, when and who to coach, how to ensure it gets relevant "airtime" in a manager's skill set, and most of all, Scottish Business Managers need to experience the power of good coaching directly, not just through mentorship from above.

And to all those CEOs who are excellent coaches – keep up the good work!

"Craniumintrarectumitis" – A Common Managers' Ailment

In today's hectic marketplace, the busy manager often suffers from a common ailment known as "craniumintrarectumitis". This condition causes managers to be always seemingly very busy, with little time for members of the team. This can be due to either being stuck with their nose in front of spreadsheets and reports, or trapped in endless, meaningless meetings. The condition can result in irrational behaviour, weight gain, irritability, loss of temper, and general malaise.

But the manager is not alone and a recent report published in the Harvard Business Review in February 2002 states:

> *"Fully, 90% of managers squander their time in all sorts of ineffective activities. A mere 10% of managers spend their time in a committed, purposeful and reflective manner"*
> ("Beware the Busy Manager" – Heike Bruch & Sumantra Ghoshal, *Harvard Business Review* February 2002)

In my experience both as a manager and as a management coach I find this to be very true, and as a result of reviewing my own experience and interviewing pharma managers, I have the found the main causes of this condition.

1. The manager's inability to plan effectively resulting in e-mail/voicemail overloads and deadlines for reports being missed. In other words the manager's lack of being able to prioritize what is important as opposed to not important.
2. The manager's inability to influence senior management, resulting in the manager performing tasks that they think

the senior management wants them to do, or, simply carrying out senior management orders despite the fact that the manager on the receiving end thinks the orders are inappropriate. This could mean attendance at non-essential meetings, irrelevant reports or inappropriate project work.

3.   The manager's belief system that says that working with projects and/or senior management /marketing is more important than working with individuals in the team. This creates a division between the team and the manager as the team feels under-valued and left out. This can mean that members of the team are not willing to come forward to take on extra work with the end result being that the manager has to do them.

4.   The manager's lack of capability in leading a team effectively, particularly in the skill of delegation.

So how does one treat this ailment so as the condition does not become terminal? The following is a five-step course of treatment can be taken not only to alleviate the symptoms, but also to actually treat the underlying causes.

1.   Get the manager to take time out and take stock of the situation. A good senior manager or coach will support the manager to identify where he or she is under pressure. Where are they spending their time? What are the real priorities? How can they change their habits?

2.   Once the priorities have been identified, the manager must be able to plan more effectively and have the capability and resolve to ensure the plan is put in place and is reviewed regularly. Again a senior manager or coach should support the manager in achieving this.

3.   Once they have taken stock and put a plan into place then the next step of the treatment is to communicate the plan and it's

contents to both senior management and the team in order to manage everyone's expectations as this plan will probably mean a change in the manager's behaviours. The manager will have to contract with senior management and the team as to what will be different from now on. (This takes courage and good feedback skills as it may mean not attending meetings or it could mean challenging the production of meaningless reports!)

4. The next step is to get buy-in from the team and to identify within the team those individuals, who are capable or potentially have the capability, to take on some of the manager's tasks. This will not only free up some of the manager's time but it will also give those capable individuals in the team that much needed extra "challenge" that should ensure they remain motivated and committed.

5. The final stage of the treatment is to ensure that regular review of the new plan and its objectives happens on a regular basis. Without this review how can the manager know whether or not the treatment is working? The manager should be doing a self-analysis and also getting feedback from the team and superiors, to check that signs of the condition are not re-appearing.

Take the full course of treatment and do regular check-ups and you will find that the common condition of "craniumintrarectumitis" can be treated successfully and also be kept at bay forever.

Making the Most out of Sales Manager Field Visits

The visit of a sales manager to a sales executive out on their "territory" should be an opportunity for growth and development for the executive, the sales manager, the organisation and the customer. More often than not, this is not the case, with the executive often dreading the visit as it is seen as purely an assessment.

Allan Mackintosh BSc FInstSMM, who has over twelve years experience of performing "field visits" with sales executives as a sales manager and sales coach, investigates the difference between a developmental and motivational field visit as opposed to one which promotes dread and fear.

There are tremendous advantages of performing field visits with sales executives. From the executive's point of view, here is a chance to impress, to let the boss see what happens in the real world, and to sit down, face to face, with the manager to review progress and to discuss career development. From the manager's perspective, the visit is a chance to observe the executive's skills, to coach them to enhanced performance, to praise, and to discuss any issues and concerns that the executive may have. From the organisation's point of view, these coaching visits by the manager should lead to increased motivation, capability and performance of the sales executive leading to increased sales results.

Why then, do field visits often produce the opposite, with executives dreading "the boss" coming out with them?

Let me take you through the four key elements of any field visit and within each I will outline what should happen and what potentially can go wrong.

1.   **Contracting**

Contracting is simply an agreement between the manager and the sales executive. Contracting should take two forms.

Firstly, a contract should be set up in terms of how the day should look. (when and where the manager meets the sales executive.) At this stage the manager should agree what his objectives are for the day in terms of how long he is going to stay with the executive and what he would like to see and discuss. The manager should also ask the executive what his or her aims are for the day in relation to both the business for the day and what they are expecting from the manager. It should be a win/win situation. This phase of contracting should happen prior to the visit.

Secondly, this contract should be revisited on the day, prior to the start of any sales calls and it should be extended to agreements around what happens in the sales call. How does the manager behave? When, where and how does he or she give feedback?

If a solid contract is agreed then both the manager's and the executive's expectations are being explored and hopefully met. Both should have the needs for the day met.

My experience has shown me that contracting does not happen as regularly or as fully as it should. Expectations tend to be one-way with the manager dictating what he or she wants to get out of the day and very little attention paid to the sales executive's needs. The sales executive sees the day as the manager coming out to assess. This puts the sales executive very much on the defensive and they then begin to structure the day to satisfy what they think is important for the manager to see, as opposed to structuring the day to get the most out of the time they have with their manager. Many sales executives will fill their day with sales calls, keeping the manager on his toes, and letting the manager see that they are "busy". What about the important review times between calls and dedicated discussion time for review-ing progress and career development?

Once a contract is agreed it must be kept, or only changed through agreement. The worst thing that can happen is that the manager breaks the contract. Broken contracts lead to mistrust.

2.   The Pre- Call

This is the vital element that will dictate just how competent a sales executive is in terms of planning the sales call both in terms of objective setting and strategy. Also, this is a chance for the manager to use their coaching skills to enable the sales executive to set specific objectives and to think through their plan of approach in order to hit the objec-tives. Time should be taken prior to each call, and the manager should support the sales executive to set S.M.A.R.T (specific, measurable, achievable, realistic, timed) objectives. Discussion and coaching should take place in order to support the executive to map out the best way for-ward for them to achieve the objectives. Challenge should also be used when objectives are not specific enough or not "stretching" enough.

All this takes time, but it is well worth it. I've seen too many managers not take the time to coach the sales executive through this stage and as a result the executive has "woolly" objectives and an unclear approach as to how to tackle and sell to the customer. The result of this can be no sales and "less than appreciative" feedback from the manager! Take the time before every call!

3.   The In-Call

This is where the sales call actually takes place. Depending on the agreed contract beforehand, the sales executive will perform the call and the manager will observe. Sometimes with new sales executives, the manager will agree to come in and support the sales presentation, but with more experienced executives, the manager should observe the sales call only. All the time whilst observing the manager should be listening intently to how the call is progressing and be observing body language of both the executive and the customer. All this information will be needed if good quality feedback is to be given after the sales call is over.

Many managers do not observe the rule of observation, even if a contract has been agreed. Some take over the call leaving the executive, and potentially the customer, frustrated. Some butt in at inappropriate moments, causing greater frustration. Keep out unless the contract you have agreed dictates that you can come in and support at appropriate times! It is the manager's responsibility to support and maintain three-way rapport.

4.   **The Post- Call Analysis**

Immediately after the sales call, time should be taken to analyse how the sales call has gone. How did the sales executive do in respect to their specific objectives? What went well, not so well? What were the manager's observations? This is the stage where the manager's skills should really come to the fore. How well can the manager coach? Do they know how to use the right coaching intervention with the right individual at the right time? How good at giving feedback are they? Do they praise enough?

A useful structure for a post-call analysis is offered by: POW! where:

P = Praise. The first thing a manager should do is praise regardless of how well the call went. Managers are too quick to jump on what didn't go well as opposed to praising what did go well.

O= Objectives and Observations. How well did the sales executive fare against their specific Objectives? Invite then to do a self-assessment of what went well and not so well. Reinforce this self-assessment and add anything relevant through your own Observations.

W = Way Forward and Will. Once an agreement has been obtained about how well the call went, coach them to greater performance next time by having them forge new objectives for that specific call together with coaching them to explore the various options available to them. Help them decide what approach is best for them and then check their Will in order to carry them out.

This stage of the field visit is the one that can cause the most damage. More often than not, managers do not praise enough. They are quick to give their opinions of what happened rather than let the sales executive explore what happened. Managers tend also to give advice as opposed to coach. "I would do it this way....it worked for me.....you try it....etc" Giving advice is necessary in some instances and the approach is dictated by the skill and the will of the sales executive that is being worked with. How many managers can coach effectively? How many use the Skill/Will Matrix to determine their coaching approach to a particular sales executive? Doing an effective post-call analysis that is developmental and motivation takes time and this can impact upon contact rates. Also, this time isn't usually built into the contract because the contract is either non-existent or "flimsy". Put time aside! This stage is crucial if the capability of the sales executive is to be increased. Managers have to build in the time and they have to have the necessary coaching skills in order for the post-call analysis to be effective.

The Managers who contract well, who coach, praise and give good quality feedback together with having a mindset of development versus assessment are the managers who look forward to field visits because of the results that can be obtained. Also these are the Managers that are welcomed on field visits by the sales executives as opposed to those that are dreaded.

What type of manager are you?

Five Secrets to Managing your Manager Productively

The biggest reason why people leave organisations is that the role they are doing is no longer offering any challenge or excitement. The second reason is due to the behaviour and capability of the immediate line manager. More often than not, the two are strongly linked with the manager taking little interest in the representative's development and as such the representative feels under valued and bored due to the lack of attention and challenge.

Often the blame is laid at the manager's door, but the representative must take a share of the responsibility also. What normally happens is that expectations are not laid out "on the table" with both parties unaware of each other's needs, motivations and expectations. The end result is often a lack of trust and respect between employee and manager which leads inevitably to conflict.

So how can you avoid this conflict and start to work productively with your manager? Act on these five secrets and watch your relationship grow.

Secret 1: Learn about behavioural styles and find out what your own is and your manager's. Compare the two and if there are differences then work on these differences by matching your manager's body language very discreetly. Match their tone and volume of voice, remembering not to mimic only discreetly match. Look at their eye movements and do similar. Again, do similar with body movements. When you start to discreetly match their body language you will be amazed that they start to match yours also. This is the start of the rapport building process and this goes a long way to start the building of trust.

Secret 2: Contract with your manager by getting agreement about how best the two of you are going to work together. Ask questions such as:

"What are your specific expectations of me as your representative?"

"What are my specific objectives and how am I going to be measured?"

"What behaviours annoy you?"

"What motivates and de-motivates you?"

"What reports do you want? When do you want them? What content?"

"How often do you want to visit me in the field?"

Contracting is all about managing expectations. A good manager will always outline his or her expectations and will ask you about yours. Once you both are clear about what each other's expectations are then this is another building block in the foundations of trust and respect.

One of the hardest lessons I learned was when I did not contract with a senior manager. We had completely opposite behavioural styles, which meant that we didn't get off to the best start. He thought I was too energetic, flighty and too much of a risk taker and I though he was too detailed with no personality and constantly stuck in front of spreadsheets. We were in constant conflict because he asked me for reports that I could see no reason for and I was frustrated when he ignored my pleas for more training budget. If we had contracted and discussed our similarities and differences and how best to work with them, we may not have had the conflict that we did have.

Secret 3: Ask for regular feedback on your progress. Ask your manager to coach and mentor you. Be pro-active and do not wait for your manager to come to you. On the other hand do not always be seen to be reliant on your manager and give them space. Agree this area of support in your contract.

Secret 4: Be seen to be a support for your manager. Management can be lonely and stressful particularly if the manager isn't managing their boss particularly well or if the company and/or team results are not doing as well as expected. Be supportive and offer to take on extra tasks. These tasks will not only make space for the manager to work more productively and strategically they will also enable you to develop your own capabilities.

Secret 5: Go with your instincts! If you feel that the relationship with your manager is starting to go sour, then immediately call a meeting and openly discuss your feelings. To make this easier than it may sound, again build it into your contract right at the start. Something like, "If I feel our relationship is not what it should be, can I address it immediately as opposed to letting it linger?"

Relationships between managers and representatives usually deteriorate because there was little trust in the first place and as a result openness is not usually achieved. Follow the five secrets and you will go a long way to ensuring a lasting and productive relationship with your manager.

Ten Steps towards a Stress-Free Management Induction

Becoming a manager for the first time can be an unnerving and sometimes stressful experience. In many cases, organizations expect you to immediately jump into the role and begin to perform as if you have been there for years! Also, you may have been promoted "out of the blue" and as such have not taken part in any "succession planning" that would have prepared you for the management role.

If you follow the ten steps that I will outline then you will put yourself in a much better position to develop into your management role than perhaps may not have been the case.

Step 1: Be yourself!

It is important that you do not try to act like your predecessor. You will have your own style of management and it may be that the previous manager had a particular style that you were not comfortable with. You will have an idea of what the best management style is for any given situation but this will only come with time, perhaps through training and coaching. The best thing you can do is to look at yourself and decide what you want out of the management role and what you need to do in order to build your capabilities in that role.

Step 2: Go easy to start with

Although there is always pressure on a new manager to take up where the last manager left off, don't go rushing into things. Do not be the "new broom that sweeps clean" all previous procedures away. Ensure that you reassure your team that it will be "business as usual" at least until you get the opportunity to speak to each team member about what their fears and hopes are as regards you being their manager.

Step 3: Talk to people, listen and gather information

It is vital that you talk to each member of your team. Sit down with them and "contract" with them. How do the two of you want to work together? What are their expectations of you as their manager? What are their hopes, fears and aspirations? What are their motivators and de-motivators? It is important that this is a two way process and you should be asking them the same questions so as there is mutual understanding. Also ask them what they think needs to be done to make the team or department more effective - seek their input right at the start.

Although it is important to talk to the team, it is also vital to talk and contract with those senior managers who will have a "stake" in your actions. They must be comfortable and if you "contract" with them as you would with your own team then you will have greater under-standing of them as they will have of you.

Step 4: Ensure you get coaching and mentoring from your own boss

Once you have established a working relationship with your own manager then ensure that within this "contract" he or she builds in time to coach and mentor you through, particularly the early day. As a new manager you should know exactly what is expected of you in terms of both your business objectives and your development objec-tives. You should have a development plan that highlights your strengths and development areas in respect to your new role and with the support of your manager you should start to implement that plan immediately. Your manager should have the coaching skills to ensure that you maintain your progress and deliver against your plan.

Step 5: Know the Boundaries, Policies and Procedures

In many "new manager" situations teams, or individuals within teams, attempt to "change the rules" in relation to what needs to be done and how it is done. There will be company rules and procedures and these need to be adhered to, until at least the time they have been reviewed and any change negotiated and implemented. Don't let you being the "new boy" be an excuse for teams or individuals to take liberties. Let people know where they stand; what they can do without asking; what they need to ask to do, and what they cannot do.

Step 6: Be Available and Visible

Make sure you are available and visible. It is very easy to be "available" over the phone or through e-mail but you cannot beat a good "face to face" very so often. It is vital to your team's development and progress that you make time to sit down with them and have regular face-to-face chats. As a manager you will be their coach and mentor and as such you should make time to coach them through their business objectives and challenges. Don't hide behind "important meetings" as many managers are apt to do.

Step 7: Avoid Favourites and Ensure Consistency and Fairness

You may be now managing the team you were once part of. You will have had friends in that team and perhaps had some people you did not get on with. You now have to ensure that you do not let your personal preferences get in the way of you effectively managing that team and the individuals within the team. Avoid favouritism at all costs and ensure you treat everyone equally, fairly and consistently. The minute you take sides the team starts to disintegrate.

Step 8: Keep communication high and as open as possible

It is important that you keep communication levels high, letting your people know what is happening whenever possible. Avoid being secretive where possible as people naturally jump to conclusions, usually the wrong ones! Make sure you praise when you see something good done. Praise is the most powerful form of feedback and unfortunately managers do not use enough of it! Consider starting a newsletter and although you instigate it and perhaps write the first couple of editions, let the team take over and start to delegate the tasks involved to the team.

Also, ensure that you ask for regular feedback from both your team and from your boss. How are getting on in relation to your new role? What do you still need to develop? What's going well?

Step 9: Be Pro-active and start to make your own decisions

Many first time managers continue to go to the "boss" to ask for permission to do things. This does not raise their profile with either senior management or with their own team. You are the boss! You can make your own decisions, so you must know what the boundaries are in relation to what you can do and what you can do. In your early contracting with your own manager ensure you know where you stand and then be pro-active about moving your business forward.

Step 10: Encourage the team to work together

The outputs of a well-disciplined and effective team will always be greater than the individual outputs of the team members and to this end you have to encourage the team to work effectively together. You have also to get them to understand that you are learning the management game and that you will need their support as well. If you can get the unit working cohesively together they will support you through your early management days.

Bonus Step! 11. Take time out to relax and reflect

In the attempts to get the job done, many new managers do not take time out to relax, wind down and then reflect on their progress. They go thrashing about from task to task never stopping to ask for feedback. This can be dangerous to their health and also to the wellbeing of the team as a whole. Make sure you take a break occasionally. Your coach and mentor will ensure that this happens – or will they?

Conclusion

You have come to the end of the *The Successful Coaching Manager*. My intention was to ensure that you as a manager and prospective manager were given enough pointers and benefits about coaching to help you get started, improve your present situation, and whet your appetite for more information. It is with my best wishes that I offer you this book to enable and support you to become a great and successful coaching manager.

Allan Mackintosh

allan@pmcscotland.com

Works Cited

Harrison,   Paul   (1996)   [online] members.aol.com/Heraklit1/zeno.htm. Zeno of Citium

Maslow, A. (1998) *Maslow on Management*. New York: John Riley & Sons, Inc.

Whitmore, John (1992). *Coaching For Performance*. Nicholas Brealey

[online] www.buzancentre.com (1996–2002) Buzan Centre for Business

[online] www.wilsonlearning.com (2002) Wilson Learning Corporation

Bibliography

I would like to acknowledge the authors of the following books whose writings have given me many ideas and inspiration during my coaching career thus far. This list is also intended to serve as a recommended reading list for anyone interested in learning more about coaching.

Belbin, Meredith R. (1981) *Management Teams – Why they Succeed or Fail*. Butterworth Heinemann

Blanchard, Ken (1994) *The One-Minute Manager Builds High Performing Teams*. Harper Collins

Bone, Diane (1988) *A Practical Guide to Effective Listening*. London Press

Cahill, Janet Ph.D., Department of Psychology, Rowan College of New Jersey Paul A. Landsbergis, Ed.D., M.P.H., Hypertension Center, Cornell University Medical College Peter L. Schnall, M.D., M.P.H., Center for Social Epidemiology

Presented at the *Work Stress and Health '95 Conference*. September 1995, Washington D.C.)

Heller, Robert & Hindle, Tim (1998) Essential Manager's Manual. Dorling Kindersley

Landsberg, Max (1996) *The Tao of Coaching*. Harper Collins

Lillibridge, E. Michael (1998) *The People Map*. Lilmat Press

Mulligan, John (1988) *The Personal Management Handbook*. Warner Books

Phillips, Nicola (1995) *Motivating for Change*. Pitman Publishing

Robbins, Harvey & Finley Michael (1995) *Why Teams Don't Work*. Pacesetter Books

Weafer, Sean (2001) *The Business Coaching Revolution*. Blackhall Publishing

Whitmore, John (1992) *Coaching For Performance*. Nicholas Brealey

About the Author

Allan Mackintosh is a Training and Development Professional with over twenty-one years experience in industry. The years he spent in the pharmaceutical industry have given him experience as a sales executive, sales manager, sales coach, and trainer. He spent six years working as a Manager / Development Coach with GlaxoWellcome and GlaxoSmithKline before branching out to form his own management coaching business in 2001. His last industry role involved coaching top-flight sales executives, first-line and senior managers, and providing support to enable them to identify and achieve their business objectives. Particular emphasis was placed on supporting new managers who had been promoted to management from the sales function. He has taken this experience and expertise and formed his own business, Performance Management Coaching.

As well as Management Coaching, Allan was heavily involved in Training. His expertise in designing and delivering training programs spans several areas:

- Sales Skills
- Communication and Influencing Skills
- Teambuilding

- Time & Stress Management
- Objective Setting & Monitoring
- Coaching Skills
- Presentation Skills
- Holding Effective meetings

Allan was also instrumental in supporting the implementation of several innovative programs for GlaxoWellcome including:

- Self- Directed Team Working
- Team & Peer Appraisals
- Action Learning Sets

In May 2001, Allan founded Performance Management Coaching. to promote the skill of coaching in business and to enable and support managers to become great coaches in the workplace. Since starting Performance Management Coaching Allan has steadily grown "The Coaching Manager" brand and it now covers an e-zine, e-book/CD-ROM and several structured courses and eCourses.